EXPLORING SPORTS SERIES

GOLF

About the author

Few persons could be better qualified to write about learning the grand game of golf than *Virginia L. Nance* (Mrs. Edward K.). She has participated in all levels of competition, from a youngster in local and junior events to the major amateur women's tournaments, including the U.S. Amateur for Women. She has been medalist, semifinalist, runner-up, and winner of many tournaments.

But Mrs. Nance has excelled even more as a teacher, giving both private and class lessons to boys and girls, men and women, in high schools, at golf-practice ranges, in camps, and at colleges and universities. She has conducted numerous clinics for students and teachers at local, state, and national levels. Mrs. Nance is a Class A Teaching and Life Member of the Ladies Professional Golf Association. She has been a contributor of articles for DGWS and AAHPER publications. She holds degrees from the University of Illinois and the University of Wisconsin and has completed further graduate work at the University of Southern California.

Dr. Elwood Craig Davis, co-author, is a well-known and distinguished professor of physical education, having been associated with major institutions such as Pennsylvania State University, University of Pittsburgh, University of Louisville, and professor emeritus at University of Southern California. His last teaching was at California State University at Northridge. His honors are legion, the most outstanding perhaps being a recipient of the Phi Epsilon Kappa National Award and both the American Academy of Physical Education's Hetherington Award and the AAHPER's Luther Halsey Gulick Medal.

Dr. Davis is a graduate of the University of Washington, University of Chicago, and Columbia University. Service was in U.S. Naval Aviation and Naval Physical Training. He is the author or coauthor of nine books and numerous articles.

EXPLORING SPORTS SERIES

GOLF

Virginia Lindblad Nance
Elwood Craig Davis

Wm. C. Brown Company Publishers
Dubuque, Iowa

Consulting Editors

Physical Education
Aileene Lockhart
Texas Woman's University

Parks and Recreation
David Gray
California State University, Long Beach

Health
Robert Kaplan
The Ohio State University

**Physical Education Activities
Evaluation Materials Editor**

Jane A. Mott
Texas Woman's University

6-18-87   Gift   3⁹⁵

Illustrations by Ruth Schonhorst and Denise Powell

Cover photo: David Lissy/Atoz Images

Copyright © 1966, 1971, 1975, 1980, 1983 by
Wm. C. Brown Company Publishers

Library of Congress Catalog Card Number: 82-82956

ISBN 0—697—09961-X

Printed in the United States of America

contents

preface

This, the fourth edition of *Golf*, continues the same dual objectives established for previous editions: to present the golf strokes in a simple but thorough way so that the reader may become a more intelligent and enlightened student of the game—better able to learn and develop skill in the strokes; and, to present information that will enable the reader to become well-grounded in the knowledges of golf as a game.

This current edition has been considerably revised and additions have been made to better accomplish these objectives.

A new feature is the GRIP-GUIDE, a pattern for learning the correct grip. With the Grip-Guide taped on the club-handle you can quickly place your hands in the proper position on the club. This guide can facilitate and accelerate your learning the correct grip, the first requirement for developing a sound swing and hitting good golf shots. The guide also serves as a check for maintaining the correct grip in practice. This device, for both the right-hander and left-hander, along with the accompanying thorough discussion of the grip should make learning and teaching this skill an easier-than-usual task for you and your instructor.

Another new feature, A Home Practice Plan, has been added. The plan is simplified so that you may adapt it to fit your needs and available time. It is a basic plan—a step toward becoming skillful in swinging a club. Many other practice suggestions presented in the book will furnish you ideas for developing a total practice program.

We have retained our original concept of presenting the golf strokes. After establishing an important base of understanding certain fundamentals of learning and some mechanics of swinging the club, we progress to learning the grip, stance, and the swings—working from the simple to the complex.

The common errors encountered by players are studied and the reader is urged to join in thinking through the causes and examining possible solutions to poor golf shots. We do not believe that players should be thoroughly mystified by shot errors and in their frustration ready to abandon the game. We believe any player can do a lot to help himself, but we also respect the importance of having a competent instructor observe the golf swing and make corrections. We, the authors, cannot see the student make the error so we readily admit our limitations.

To accomplish the second purpose of the book—to become well-grounded in the knowledges of the game—we continue to aim for a complete and thorough coverage of the rules of etiquette and safety, the golf rules, and an extensive glossary of golf terms—plus test materials which evaluate your knowledge of golf. Our ultimate aim is that you become a golfer—a person who enjoys the game and contributes to making the game enjoyable for other players, who respects the rights of others and realizes the course is shared with other golfers, who abides by the etiquette and rules of the game.

This book is intended to be a supplement to golf instruction. Because so many theories about the golf swings exist, no single book could be all-inclusive. The reader should not conclude that concepts and ideas left out of this book are necessarily questioned or rejected.

We wish to express our appreciation to the teachers and golfers who have given us their comments and criticisms. We have carefully studied their suggestions and incorporated some of them.

We hope the presentations made in this book on the skills and knowledges of the game will contribute to your making golf a lifetime recreation.

the game of golf

1

Golf is a game, a profession, a business asset, a social activity, and often a humiliating experience. The "put-down" that golf renders to all players may be its fascination. Golf teases you. It can lift you into ecstatic worlds where you dream of playing perfect golf. Then without warning your dreams are shattered—golf has put you in your place. Time and again the game seems to delight in proving that you can only be its devotee—not its master. After your visions of playing great golf are dimmed, you manage to stroke some shots with unusual skill. Again you are coaxed back into the imaginary world of perfect golf. Such is the lure of golf—sampling the joy of hitting fine shots, followed by great hopes, disappointments, and renewed hopes. The spirit and desire to attempt to conquer this challenging game survive despite all of its vicissitudes.

You are either one of the millions of people playing golf or you soon will be. It is not necessary to "sell" golf. The advantages of knowing how to play are evident. Ever-increasing numbers of people choose to learn golf and once chosen, golf becomes an enjoyable, lifetime recreation.

THE GAME

The object of golf is to play a round, usually 18 holes, in as few strokes as possible. At the beginning of each hole you are allowed to tee the ball so it is slightly elevated from the turf. After you strike the ball from the tee, you must then play the ball as you find it (except as otherwise provided in the rules), and continue doing so, in your turn, until you hit the ball into the hole (cup) which is sunk in a carpet-like area known as the *putting green*. A *flagstick* is placed in the center of the cup so that the position of the hole can be seen from a distance. Some courses will have the hole number printed on the pennant of the flagstick.

The area of closely mowed grass between the tee and the putting green is called the *fairway*. The game would be relatively simple if you had to only

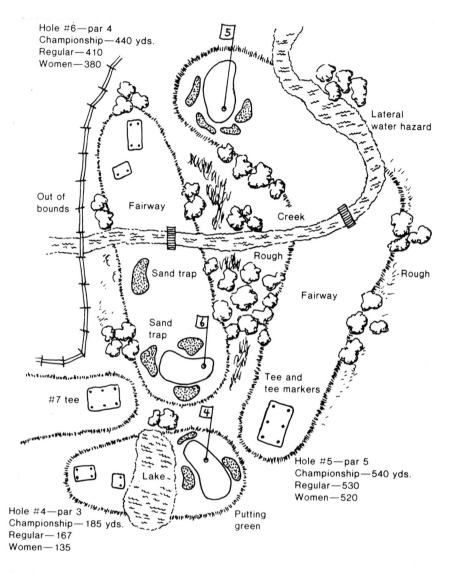

Hole #6—par 4
Championship—440 yds.
Regular—410
Women—380

Lateral
water hazard

Out of
bounds

Fairway

Creek

Rough

Sand trap

Rough

Fairway

Sand
trap

Tee and
tee markers

#7 tee

Hole #5—par 5
Championship—540 yds.
Regular—530
Women—520

Lake

Hole #4—par 3
Championship—185 yds.
Regular—167
Women—135

Putting
green

Fig. 1.1   Three golf holes

play the ball from the tee, the fairway, and the putting green. But such is not the case. If you hit a shot off line and off the fairway, you are likely to find your ball among trees and in long, thick grass—the *rough*. Because of a poorly hit or misjudged shot your ball may land in a *hazard*, such as a creek, lake, or sand trap. You can be sure that, thanks to these and other possible occurrences, playing the game of golf will test your skill and your character. (fig. 1.1)

Define or describe these areas of a golf course: tee, fairway, hazards, rough, and putting green.

After you complete play of each hole you record the number of strokes you have taken on a score card (see Etiquette—Putting Green). You add your scores for each nine holes and then total these figures for your 18-hole score. (fig. 1.2).

Play U.S.G.A. Rules except as modified by Local Rules.   Please Observe Rules of Etiquette.

	1	2	3	4	5	6	7	8	9	OUT	10	11	12	13	14	15	16	17	18	IN	TOTAL	HDCP	NET
Yards - Championship - Blue	525	430	405	185	540	440	160	380	440	3505	505	420	180	535	455	210	400	435	442	3582	7087		
Regular White	510	415	400	167	530	410	150	370	420	3372	490	385	165	520	423	185	375	415	428	3386	6758		
PAR	5	4	4	3	5	4	3	4	4	36	5	4	3	5	4	3	4	4	4	36	72		
Handicap*	11	5	15	7	9	1	13	17	3		10	16	14	8	2	12	18	6	4				
HOLE	1	2	3	4	5	6	7	8	9	OUT	10	11	12	13	14	15	16	17	18	IN	TOTAL	HDCP	NET
Yards - Women Red	480	375	395	135	520	380	147	365	380	3177	470	360	140	510	375	180	370	395	415	3215	6392		
PAR	5	4	4	3	5	4	3	4	4	36	5	4	3	5	4	3	4	4	5	37	73		
Handicap*	5	13	1	17	3	11	7	15	9		8	12	18	6	16	4	14	2	10				

Date _____   Scorer _____   Attest _____

Course Rating** Men 69.8 - Women 70.6

Please Replace Divots....Repair Ball Marks on Greens....Rake Sand Traps

Slow Players Must Allow Following Group To Play Through

*Handicap—These numbers indicate the ranking of the golf holes in order of difficulty. Hole #6, HDCP. rating #1, is considered the most difficult hole for men. Hole #3 is rated the most difficult for women. Holes #16 and #12, HDCP. rating #18 for men and women respectively, are considered the least difficult.

**Course Rating—Evaluation of the playing difficulty of a course compared with other rated courses.

Fig. 1.2   Score card

Par—The Ever-Present Opponent

Par scores are good scores. The score card shows the par for each hole, the total for each 9-holes, and the 18-hole total. When you play you can always match your scores against these par figures.

The major guide in determining par for a hole is the distance of the hole. The number of strokes a good player needs to hit the ball onto the putting green is figured, and then two strokes are added for play on the green. On the average, men hit the ball farther than women do, so women's par will differ from men's par on some of the holes.

COMPUTATION OF PAR

	Women		Men
Par		Par	
3	up to 210 yards	3	up to 250 yards
4	211-400	4	251-470
5	401-575	5	471 and over
6	576 and over		

A Challenge Requiring Self-Discipline and Concentration

Even though you usually play in a group of four, golf is a personal game. From the time you hit the ball off the first tee until you remove it from the cup on the eighteenth green you are in command of your own game. You do not react to a moving ball someone else has hit or thrown as in tennis or softball. Nongolfers may scoff at the game: "What's so difficult about hitting a ball that is sitting still? . . . after all you know where the ball is and can position yourself to hit it." You can bet these same people will question the sense of such statements when they try to hit a ball that lies so still. In golf if the ball is missed completely or is hit poorly, you cannot dismiss the incident by saying the opponent hit a superb shot. Allowed no excuses, you must face the inert ball again. But when you hit excellent shots, the game rewards you—you can claim credit for fine play.

You perform in a silent atmosphere, sensitive to everything both inside and outside yourself. Having time to think and act in quiet surroundings adds a singular dimension—one demanding concentration and self-discipline. No shot is played without some thought. This is not so in many games where brilliant plays may be or must be executed as a result of rapid-fire reaction only. You must plan the play, control your thinking, initiate and complete the action in order to play each shot. You have time to be introspective—which can be either a detriment or an advantage. You can "talk" yourself into a bad shot, or a good shot.

All players admire and respect the skill of the tournament professionals, but in the last analysis the most important subject of thought and conversation for each golfer is: "My game."

GOLF COURSES

Much expert knowledge and work go into planning, building, and maintaining a golf course. Sometimes the playing of the game is so absorbing or exasperating that the beauty and design of a golf course are forgotten momentarily. Golf requires the largest playing field of any modern game. All courses and all holes differ. The architect designs the course to challenge you to hit your best shots and to penalize you if you fail to do so. He lays out the course taking full advantage of the topography, the beauty of nature and of the outdoors.

On what may be called standard courses, holes vary in length from about 100 yards to about 600 yards. Since golf does not have an exact regulation playing field, the golfer must continually adapt his game to the peculiarities of each course, which may in itself vary in length and challenge from day to day. To protect the turf on the teeing area and around the cup on the putting green, the tee markers and the cups are shifted often. If the teeing areas and putting greens are large, placement of both tee markers and cups can make a significant difference in the difficulty and the lengths of the holes.

Some golf courses have unusually long teeing areas or have more than one tee per hole. On these courses three sets of tee markers may be set up:

blue markers for the back tees—the championship course; white markers for the middle tees—the regular course; and, red markers for the front tees—the women's course. (The colors of the markers may vary from course to course.) Many courses have only two sets of tees, regular and women's tees.

The changing of the cups on the putting greens from flat to various undulating surfaces adds challenge and zest to the game. On many courses, especially those bordering the ocean or in the mountains, the ball may roll over the slanting surfaces in a direction exactly opposite to the one decided on by the player. There is a story that after one man played an ocean-side course for the first time, he became so frustrated trying to figure out the roll of the ball on the greens that he returned the next day with a carpenter's level to check the slopes of the putting greens. (The rules of golf do not permit the use of such a device.)

Courses having all short holes offer certain advantages to the novice. A simpler version of golf is played, thus more success and pleasure are possible for the beginners. For all players these short courses are challenging, offer practice in the important short game, and require less time for the completion of a round.

Golf is not all of life, but to have the opportunity to play outstandingly beautiful and ability-testing courses throughout the world is enriching life for an increasing number of people.

GOLF CLUBS

You are permitted to carry a maximum of fourteen clubs when you play golf. All players do not use a full set, and players using a full set do not all select the same clubs. However, the usual set of fourteen clubs consists of one putter, nine irons, and four woods.

Putter

This club is carried by every golfer, and it is the one club used most often. You use the putter to roll the ball relatively short distances into the hole It is used principally on the putting green and from near it. The putter has a short shaft and an almost vertical face. Aside from these two points there is great variation in the design and construction of putters: the shaft may be attached to any part of the clubhead; the size and contour of the grip may be different than the standard grip of the woods and irons; the clubhead may be constructed in a variety of shapes.

Fig. 1.3   Types of putters

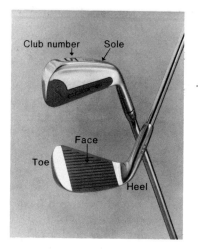

Fig. 1.4   Parts of clubhead

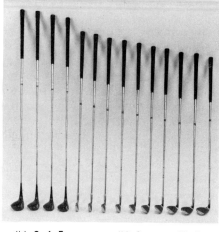

#1, 3, 4, 5   #2-9   Wedges
Woods   Irons   Pitching
                       and sand

Fig. 1.5   Irons and woods.

#3   #5   #7   #9   Wedge   #1   #3   #4   #5
                                  Driver

Fig. 1.6   Club-face loft—irons   Fig. 1.7   Club-face loft—woods

Photographs of irons and woods courtesy of Cobra Golf, Inc., San Diego, California

Irons

Matched sets of irons consist of either eight or nine clubs: the eight-club set includes the irons numbered 3 through 9, plus a wedge; the nine-club set consists of the irons numbered 2 through 9, plus a wedge. The #2-iron (or the #3 in the 3-9 set) has the longest shaft and the least club-face loft. As the club number goes up—4, 5, 6, etc., the shaft decreases in length, the angle of the club-face loft increases, and the distance obtainable decreases. There is a great variation in the distances and the trajectories of the golf shots that can be hit with the different irons. The distance differential between each of the irons is approximately ten yards. If you can hit a ball 130 yards with a 5-iron, you then can figure that you should hit a 4-iron shot 140 yards, and a 6-iron shot 120 yards.

The wedge has a heavier head and greater loft than the #9-iron. The club may be a pitching, sand, or dual purpose wedge. Some matched sets contain both a pitching and a sand wedge.

Besides the wedges, other special irons are made for hitting the ball short distances. Irons with medium loft and relatively short shafts are used to play low trajectory shots (run-up or chip shots) to the putting green. These clubs are marketed under various names but are generally called chipping irons.

In the past irons were referred to by name, e.g., #5—mashie, #9—niblick. Today you will seldom hear any numbered iron called by name.

Woods

Matched sets of woods are usually made up of four clubs, numbers 1, 3, 4, and 5. Formerly, the 2-wood was included in all sets, but because of its limited usefulness it has declined in popularity. The shafts of the woods are longer than those of the irons so you can expect to hit the ball farther with these clubs than with the irons. Like the irons, the different numbered woods vary in shaft length and club-face loft. The almost vertical face of the driver restricts its use to hitting the ball from a tee. There is a distance differential of approximately 10 yards between each of the different numbered woods.

Special woods having greater loft than the number 5 wood are available. Golfers who find it difficult to hit long irons prefer to use the more lofted woods instead of the irons. The numbers 1 and 3 woods are referred to by both number and name—driver (1) and spoon (3). However, the trend is to refer to all clubs, except the putter and wedge, by number.

Beginner's Set

An excellent set of clubs for the novice consists of seven clubs: putter, numbers 3, 5, 7, and 9 irons, and numbers 1 and 3 woods. A five-club set, eliminating the 1-wood and 9-iron, also makes a suitable set for the beginner. (For information on club selection, see chapter 10.)

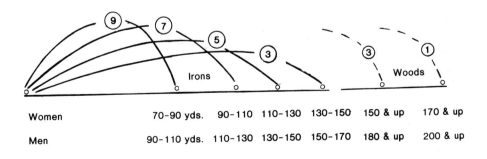

| | | 70-90 yds. | 90-110 | 110-130 | 130-150 | 150 & up | 170 & up |

Women — 70-90 yds., 90-110, 110-130, 130-150, 150 & up, 170 & up

Men — 90-110 yds., 110-130, 130-150, 150-170, 180 & up, 200 & up

Fig. 1.8   Range of approximate distances—average golfers.

safety—your most important lesson
2

Golf is a relatively safe game, but when accidents do occur they can be serious. Most accidents happen because players are careless or uninformed on safety rules. You have a *responsibility* for your safety and the safety of others. Learn the following rules and *take no chances where safety is concerned.*

1. If you are a member of an instructional class, follow the precautions given you.
2. Before you swing any club, check to see that no one is close to being within range of your swing.
3. When someone swings a club, be careful where you stand or walk. Stay well out of range of any swing.
4. Do not swing a club so that the follow-through is directed toward anyone. A divot or an unseen pebble or rock might be hit and propelled toward someone. Also, though it is not likely to happen, the club could break or it could slip out of your hands.
5. Do not stand or walk ahead of a player taking a stroke that may endanger you. Similarly, when you are about to hit a ball that could endanger someone, make sure that no one is standing or walking ahead of you.
6. Before playing any stroke on the course, make certain the group ahead is well out of range of your intended shot. Before attempting to play a shot to the putting green, wait until the group ahead has left the green and is safely out of range. An errant shot in the direction of players walking off the green can endanger them. When your group completes play on the green, replace the flagstick, and leave the green immediately. (See Etiquette—Putting Green)
7. If you hit a ball that travels toward someone and may endanger that person, call "FORE!" quickly and loudly so that he will be alerted.
8. At the practice range, stay on the tee line. Do not walk ahead of the line to retrieve balls or tees.
9. When someone is teaching you or you are teaching another player, stand opposite this person, facing him. Do not stand on his right or left side in the path of the swing.

10. A golf course is one of several locations that is extremely hazardous during lightning and thunderstorms. The best precaution to follow is to avoid playing when such storms occur. The USGA rule book contains a special section entitled, *Protection of Persons against Lightning,* which all players should read and follow.

11. If you use a motorized cart to drive around the course, drive with care and follow the course rules for operation of the cart.

Summarize into one general precaution the specific safety rules that apply to a player about to hit the ball.

Many people carry personal liability insurance for protection in case accidents do happen. The protection offered by these policies may merit your investigation and consideration.

To make golf a safe game for yourself and for other players, follow the safety precautions, be alert, and use common sense.

on learning the golf swings

3

The adult student often wants to know "how" to swing a golf club. He wants to know the intricate details of the swing—the complex analysis of the movement. Even if such an analysis were possible, what then? A full golf swing takes about two seconds. In that time how much can you think about and translate into action? Fortunately, we do not have to send conscious messages to all involved body parts at the correct split second to make a golf swing. If this were necessary, none of us could swing a golf club successfully.

FOCUSING ON DETAILS CAN SLOW YOUR PROGRESS

Questions on whether the swing is natural or unnatural are meaningless. People of all ages, even those with physical handicaps, have learned to swing a golf club well. Some people have difficulty in learning the golf swings, but the problem is not in the movement. Attempting to execute the "how" by performing many details of action is one of the chief causes of learning difficulties. Trying to think of and perform many parts of the swing in two seconds is impossible and frustrating.

Emphasizing even one detail while swinging causes trouble. No one questions that the left arm remains fairly straight during a swing (putting excepted). When the cue, "straight left arm" is carried beyond easy extension to an incorrect *stiff* position, the motion of swinging is restricted. Overemphasizing any detail can become an error that limits or distorts the whole swing.

TRUST YOUR NATIVE ABILITY FOR COORDINATION

Purpose is an important factor in determining the form of a motion. Suppose you wish to throw a ball straight up into the air. Your arm swings up sharply and your weight shifts upward with the motion. This coordination occurs without thought. You neither think of swinging your arm up nor of shifting your weight upward. Rather, you think of throwing the ball straight up into the air—and you do it!

Concentrating on the objective of the stroke—*striking the ball to a target by swinging the club in a circular pattern*—will help you learn the golf swing. Many particulars of the swing that you may now think are necessary "hows" will occur. They will take their places as part of the whole movement. In learning the golf swings, do not only try to intellectualize the process. *Permit learning to take place.* Place some trust in your body's ability to coordinate many details. Golf is not unique among sports in this regard.

SOME BASIC SWING CONCEPTS

Understanding certain mechanical principles of clubhead action is important. Yet, many players make the mistake of ignoring such information. Instead of directing their attention to the clubhead, they focus their thinking upon what to do with some body part: head, shoulder, hip, knee, ad infinitum. If a ball is hit poorly they may work on changing the movement of some body part, rather than examining the trouble source—club-face and ball contact. Simple concepts of *swing pattern, club-face and ball contact,* and *clubhead speed and distance* are guideposts for swinging a golf club well and hitting good golf shots.

1. Swing Pattern.

When you look at a golf swing you may make an incorrect interpretation of its pattern. For instance, when you look at the front view of a swing (fig. 3.1), it appears that the clubhead path is upward on the back-swing and follow-through. If, after viewing this picture, you decide that you should swing the clubhead straight back and up, you will make an incorrect and awkward movement. (The truth is that when you start the swing, rather than swinging the clubhead up, you should swing it back close to the ground).

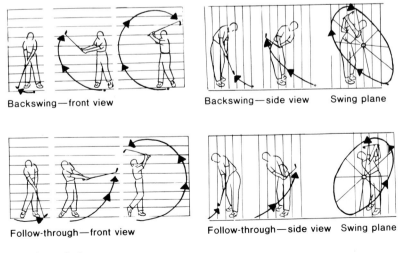

Backswing—front view   Backswing—side view   Swing plane

Follow-through—front view   Follow-through—side view Swing plane

Fig. 3.1   Swing arc

The golf swing is three-dimensional. To get a complete picture, look at the side-views of the swing. (fig. 3.1) Note that the clubhead is swung in a path gradually up and around you—it is a circular pattern on an inclined plane.

The clubhead will follow a path of least resistance. The arc described by the clubhead may be a normal outcome of swinging the club to strike the ball from the ground to a distant target.

Having correct images of how the clubhead swings through the impact zone is also important. With relation to the ground, *the clubhead travels close to the grass before and after ball contact.* With relation to the intended line of ball flight, *the clubhead enters the contact area from inside the line of flight; travels on the intended line of flight through the impact area; and, on the follow-through travels inside the intended line of ball flight.* (fig. 3.2) This is the result of the clubhead travelling in an arc around you.

2. Club-Face and Ball Contact.

The direction and flight of the ball can be directly related only to the contact of the club-face with the ball. Other factors may affect this contact, but they in themselves do not propel the ball—only the club-face can do that. If at ball contact the clubhead is travelling on the intended line of ball flight, and if the face is at right angles to that line, the ball will travel straight along the intended path to the target. The factors determining the direction the ball will travel are: (a) *the clubhead path,* and (b) *the club-face position with relation to the clubhead path.* (fig. 3.3)

A struggling golfer may say: "I can't get the ball up," or "I can't get under the ball." Until this person stops trying to propel the ball upward his troubles will continue and probably increase. When a ball is hit properly, the slant of the club-face will determine the trajectory of the ball. *You do not attempt to hit the ball into the air.* This understanding is basic to your hitting good golf shots—*try to hit the ball squarely with the club-face,* and the club-face, not an effort on your part, will loft the ball into flight.

Golf requires a high degree of accuracy. A small error in club and ball contact may cause a great error in shot result. You will get various results in early attempts to strike the ball. This should not discourage or frustrate you.

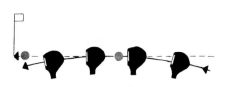

Fig. 3.2   Path of clubhead
through contact area.

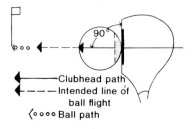

Fig. 3.3   Impact producing
straight shot to target.

Considering the size of the golf ball and the small hitting surface of the club-face, it is a wonder that so many fine golf shots are made.

3. Clubhead Speed and Distance

A typical mistake of a golfer is trying to swing faster and "harder" when for instance, he changes from hitting the ball with a #7-iron to hitting with a #5-iron. He knows that he should hit the ball approximately twenty yards farther with the #5-iron so he "feels" that he must add something to the swing to achieve the extra distance. He should not change his swing. The player should trust the longer club (with less club-face loft) to produce the extra distance.

You will avoid one of golf's common swing errors if you can be convinced that the longer club—not an extra effort on your part—produces more clubhead speed (and thus more distance). Assume that your hands move at the same rate of speed in swinging a #7-iron and a #5-iron. Because of the longer shaft, the clubhead arc traversed by the #5-iron will be greater than the one by the #7-iron, yet the elapsed time for both swings will be the same. Therefore, the clubhead of the #5-iron travelled at a greater rate of speed. The #5-iron clubhead covered more distance than the #7-iron clubhead in an equal amount of time. You will learn through practice what is the optimum rate at which you can swing to achieve the best results in both distance and accuracy. The timing and smooth blending of forces that come with correct muscular action, together with the size of the swing arc, produce *club-head speed and distance—and accuracy*. Don't take the chance of destroying a good swing by applying extra efforts and *"force"* to get distance. Trust the longer swing arcs to produce greater speed and in turn longer distances.

Should you swing "harder" for long distance shots? Should you concentrate on trying to hit the ball up into the air?

LEARNING BY IMITATION

You cannot help but use your ability to imitate in learning golf. You will "absorb" to varying degrees the golf swings you see. Imitation can be either an aid or a hindrance to learning. Young people imitate easily and to a high degree. Unlike some adults, they do not imitate on the intellectual or analytical level, but rather on a "subconscious" level. They grasp the *movement as a whole*. Pictures and feelings are registered, but not in words. Many caddies and young people have imitated fine golf swings, and this has played a part in their becoming good golfers.

Whether or not you possess a great deal of imitative ability, you can learn to make the best use of that which you have. Just as important, you can avoid complicating your learning by poor imitation. When you watch a golf swing, do not look for or try to copy small points of style, minor details of motion, or mannerisms and idiosyncracies. Keep in mind that *the golf swing is one motion*. If you see and have a "feel" for the whole of a good swing—its pattern, timing, and ease—then imitation can be an aid to learning.

PROGRESSION IN LEARNING THE SWINGS

Champion golfers prepare to play a round of golf by starting their practice using the medium or short irons. They hit shots requiring less than the full swing and then work to the longer swings and the longer clubs. This makes sense. The short swing is an important stroke of the game. The "feel" and touch for all golf swings is best found and recovered in these short strokes. Short swings serve as easy muscle and joint "warm-up" for the full swing.

The foregoing statements may be used to support this opinion: *if* it is best to start learning golf with a particular swing, then the choice should be the small swing. It is not suggested that the beginner delay working on the longer swings but patience is recommended—walk before you run. You are apt to have more success in striking the ball with the less complex short swing than with the full swing. Success in striking the ball makes learning more enjoyable as well as more effective. The putting stroke can be learned and practiced right along with the other strokes.

THE REAL SECRET

Useful guides can be given for learning golf and executing the swings, but no exact formula can be proposed. Who can confidently say he has all the answers to learning golf or to consistently hitting fine golf shots? The novice watches the champion, notes a detail of the swing, and hopefully thinks he has "discovered the secret" of good golf. Of one thing you can be sure—the champion does not want to know this *secret!* The champion already knows the REAL SECRET:—*following the fundamentals of good form in the grip, stance, and swing—and hitting thousands of golf balls in practice and play.*

You must learn the golf swing as you have learned other physical skills—through repetition. Through trial and error, and trial and success, you will discard unsuccessful swing actions and record successful swings in your "muscle memory"—and in your subconscious. You can develop an effective golf swing only through following the basics of good form and swinging a club many times.

addressing the ball
4

Taking the correct grip and the proper stance are the essential preliminary steps in executing successful golf shots with the irons and woods. Some shots may be hit well when it appears that the fundamentals of grip and stance are defied, but defiance of the fundamentals only serves to tear apart a swing, because compensations must be made constantly to counteract the incorrect positions. Give yourself the best chance to develop a sound swing and game by starting with the correct grip and stance.

THE GRIP

Types of Grips

The overlapping grip is the most widely used. In this grip, the little finger of the right hand rests on or overlaps the index finger of the left hand. In the interlocking grip the little finger of the right hand and the index finger of the left hand interlock. One advantage of either of these two positions is that there is a feeling of unity between the hands because of the overlapping or interlocking of the fingers. An advantage claimed for the overlapping grip is that you have both index fingers on the shaft. The index fingers and the thumbs are key components in holding anything. A person with small hands and short fingers may prefer the interlocking grip. Various names have been given the grip in which all the fingers of both hands are placed on the club. One claim made for this grip is that it is a strong one. The person who lacks grip strength or who has small hands may find the 10-finger grip most suitable. Individual preference, "feel," strength, and the size of hands may all be factors in choosing the best grip for you.

The three positions are much alike; the only difference between them is the placement of the little finger of the right hand and the index finger of the left hand. All three grips have been used successfully; however, the overlapping grip is favored by the majority of golfers.

Overlapping   Interlocking   "10-finger"

Fig. 4.1   Types of grips

Taking the Correct Grip*

Fig. 4.2

Fig. 4.3

Left Hand

1. Place the club sole flat on the ground and support the tip of the handle with your right hand.
2. Let your left hand hang at your side. Feel the easy hanging position of the left hand and arm.
3. Without changing the natural hanging position of the left hand, move it forward to the club so that the club handle extends across the middle section of the index finger and back across the palm (fig. 4.2). The hand, arm, and shoulder should still be in an easy, relaxed position.
4. The back of the left hand faces the intended line of ball flight. Be certain of this. Do not have the back of the left hand facing the ground with the palm pointing skyward.
5. Keeping the left hand in this proper position and relaxed, close the fingers and take hold of the club handle (fig. 4.3). Hold the club with some firmness, but not with tension. Holding the club with the left hand, you should be able to move the clubhead easily. Try moving the clubhead just a few inches back and forth on the ground while maintaining this correct grip.

*To speed up your learning of the golf grip, use the GRIP-GUIDE pattern at end of Chapter 4.

Fig. 4.4

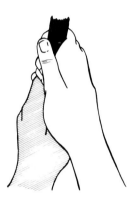

Fig. 4.5

Fig. 4.6   Left-hand grip

Right Hand
1. Let the right arm hang easily at your side. Note its natural hanging position.
2. Without changing the easy hanging position of the right hand, move the hand to the club so that the club handle lies across the middle part of the index finger. The life line of the right palm is superimposed over the left thumb (fig. 4.4).
3. The palm of the right hand faces the direction of the intended target. The palms of the hands face each other. The right hand, arm, and shoulder should still be in an easy position.
4. Close the fingers and palm of the right hand and take hold of the club (fig. 4.5). If you are taking the overlapping grip, allow the little finger of the right hand to fall naturally over the index finger of the left hand. If you are taking the interlocking grip, raise the index finger of the left hand and interlock it with the little finger of the right hand. It is important that you do not change the positions of the hands when you overlap or interlock the fingers.
5. Check the face of the club to see that it is square to the intended line of ball flight. Check the firmness of the grip and ease of motion by moving the clubhead a few inches back and forth along the ground.

Check Points — Left Hand Take hold of the club, look down at your grip, and check the following numbered points (fig. 4.6).
1. The **V** formed by the thumb and index finger points in the general area between the chin and the right shoulder. Checking where the **V** points is a matter of judgment. Follow your instructor's specific instructions.
2. The base segment of the thumb will touch the side of the hand, forming a line.
3. The left thumb is slightly to the right of a center line along the shaft.
4. The knuckles at the base of the first two fingers can be seen, and perhaps the knuckle at the base of the third finger.
5. The tip of the thumb and tip of the index finger will lie close to each other.

Fig. 4.7   Complete grip

Check Points—Right Hand (fig. 4.7)

1. The **V** formed by the thumb and index finger points in the general area between the chin and right shoulder. See left hand grip.
2. The base segment of the thumb will touch the side of the hand, forming a line.
3. The thumb is placed slightly to the left of a center line along the shaft.
4. The knuckle at the base of the index finger can be seen, and perhaps also the knuckle at the base of the long finger.
5. The tip of the thumb and the tip of the index finger lie close to each other. The tip of the thumb does not extend down the shaft beyond the middle segment of the index finger.
6. The left thumb fits in the life line of the right palm.

The left hand acts as a combination finger and palm grip. The right hand is mainly a finger grip.

The hands should feel like a single unit since they must work together.

Taking the correct grip is a basic and new skill to learn. Approach the learning in a relaxed manner. You may feel and say, "The grip is uncomfortable." You would be more correct to say that the grip is new and different. For some people, a grip that seems "comfortable" at an early stage in learning may not be a correct one. It does not follow, however, that the grip should feel awkward and difficult—it is new and so will not feel as easy as holding a pencil.

The grip is for control, touch, and speed. Do not be misled by a feeling of not having a "good hold" on the club. A vise-like, tight grip makes swinging the club impossible. Holding the club with authority is necessary, but this authority is for swinging the club, not for crushing the shaft! Hold the club with the fingers and hands. Do not tense up other parts of the body as you grip the club.

The grip should remain the same *throughout* the swing. Avoid any tendency to release the hold on the club with the last three fingers of the left hand.

Be careful that you do not develop blisters on your hands and fingers. Wearing a glove on the left hand or gloves on both hands may provide some protection.

Relation of Hand Position to Directional Flight of Ball

The position of the hands on the club affects the directional flight of the ball. For instance, if the right hand is placed on the club so that the palm points skyward, the ball is likely to travel to the left of the target. The reason for this can be easily demonstrated. Grip the club with the right hand with the palm facing skyward and the club face square to the intended target. Keeping the same hold on the club, turn the right hand so the palm faces the intended line of ball flight. Note that the club face turns over and is in a closed position pointing to the left and downward. If either or both hands are placed on the club contrary to the easy hanging position, there will be a tendency for the hand or hands to return to the natural position during the swing, thereby changing the face of the club. (See Ch. 9, Fig. 9.8)

Hand position will not always determine the directional flight of the ball because various compensations and efforts may be made during the swing to affect the club face.

When your game has developed to the point where you have a consistent stroke, you may at times wish to curve the ball to the right or left. A change in the grip could accomplish this for you. Changing the grip from the correct to the incorrect for eliminating errors in ball flight, however, is not recommended.

THE STANCE

Types of Stances

Stances are classified by drawing a relationship between the intended line of ball direction and an imaginary line extending across the front edge of the toes. These two lines are parallel in the *square stance*, the one most widely used. Taking a stance with the lines across the toes, hips, and shoulders parallel to the target line is a natural position to assume.

If the stance is changed to an *open* or *closed* one for certain shots, the change should be slight. A square stance is recommended for most golf shots.

Stances vary in width for a logical reason—the width of the stance should fit the purpose of the swing. If you wish to hit a ball a long distance, your feet are placed approximately as far apart as your shoulders are wide. This stance will allow you to swing the club in a wide arc and to keep your balance while swinging the clubhead swiftly. If you wish to hit the ball a short distance you will swing the club in a small, controlled arc, and a narrow stance fits this purpose best. The same principle applies to the distance you stand

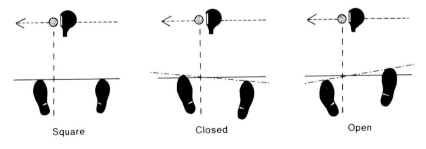

Square   Closed   Open

Fig. 4.8   Types of stances.

How does the stance differ for long and short shots? How can you determine how far to stand away from the ball?

from the ball. For distance shots, using the longer-shafted clubs, you will necessarily stand farther from the ball than you will for the shorter distance shots.

Taking the Stance

1. Aiming (Step 1, figs. 4.9 and 4.10)

   Visualize the shot you desire. Sight to the target. Draw an imaginary line through the ball to the target.

   Holding the club correctly, place the club sole flat on the ground back of the ball. The club-face points to the intended target. The edge of the clubhead where the sole and face meet should be perpendicular to the intended line of flight.

2. Placing the Feet (Step 2, figs. 4.9 and 4.10)

   When you place the clubhead back of the ball with the arms easily extended, you establish the distance you should stand from the ball. After this positioning of the club you are ready to move your feet into the correct stance.

   For a short approach shot take a comfortable narrow stance. An open stance may be preferred for this shot.

   For a wood shot, move your feet out to a comfortable stance of approximately shoulder width.

   The position of the ball in relation to the feet may vary. For most long shots the unanimous recommendation is to play the ball approximately opposite a point inside the left heel. For shorter shots the ball may be played from near this spot to a point extending toward the center of the stance. (fig. 4.11)

Step 1   Step 2

Fig. 4.9 Taking stance for short approach shot.

Step 1   Step 2

Fig. 4.10 Taking stance for wood shot.

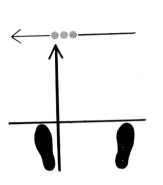

Fig. 4.11   Ball position area.

Wood shot   Short iron shot

Fig. 4.12   Addressing the ball—side view.

Check Points—The Stance

1. The left arm and the club shaft are approximately in a straight line. Let the arms hang from the shoulders. Do not try to hold the arms "stiff." The right shoulder will be slightly lower than the left because the right hand is placed below the left on the grip.
2. The hands are either slightly ahead (left of) or above the ball. As you look down at the hands it may appear that the hands are in a position left of the clubhead.
3. The toes are turned out slightly and the weight is about evenly distributed between the feet.. The knees are slightly bent.
4. The body is bent forward from the hip joints and the back is fairly straight, but not rigid. Avoid slumping and rounding the shoulders.
5. For long shots place the feet approximately shoulder width apart. For short shots take a narrow stance. Align the feet, hips, and shoulders parallel to the intended target line for the square stance. To take an open stance for the short shot, turn the left foot out and draw it back slightly.
6. The ideal position for striking most golf shots is in an area of a few inches—extending from a point opposite the inside of the left heel to a point nearly opposite the center of the stance.

THE WAGGLE AND FORWARD PRESS

A waggle is a movement of the *clubhead* in preparation for swinging the club—a rehearsal for starting the backswing. After the stance is taken the clubhead is moved away from the ball a short distance in the correct backswing path. Then it is moved forward to the ball and back to the address position. This gives you a "feel" of the club and a feeling of ease and confidence for starting the swing. The action of picking the club up and setting it down is not a waggle. Such nervous actions should be avoided.

A forward press is a movement of the body in preparation for beginning the swing. Just before the swing is started there is a slight "rocking" of weight to the left leg, accompanied by a slight bend of the right knee toward the left. Thus the name of the action—a press forward. Some golfers find that this slight shift forward helps them start the swing. Other players of varying skill do not use a forward press, or if they do the movement is so subtle that it can be scarcely seen.

The waggle and the forward press are not necessary actions, but rather auxiliary ones.

PRACTICE SUGGESTIONS

1. Practice taking the grip. Place your hands on the club, check the grip, then release your hold on the club. Repeat this action until the correct grip becomes routine. By applying the check-points and using the GRIP-GUIDE you can be confident that you will take and maintain a correct hold on the club.

2. In your early practice of taking the grip, follow the steps in the text: (a) place the left hand on the grip and check the hand position. (b) then place the right hand on the club and check the complete grip. The grip will become comfortable and easy with practice. After practice in taking the grip in two steps, take the grip almost simultaneously with both hands. Have a feeling of the two hands working together and fitting together on the club. After you check the hand positions and find them correct, then without changing the position, take a firm hold on the club.

3. Holding the club correctly, practice moving the clubhead in the air in various patterns. Write your name with the clubhead, draw circles with the clubhead, etc. Learn to feel control of the clubhead. (fig. 9.1a) These exercises are a good test of the grip in action. The wrists and arms must be relaxed and flexible while the correct hold on the club is maintained. Note that as you direct your attention to moving the clubhead, the wrists and arms move—a responsive action resulting from moving the clubhead.

4. Do exercises to develop grip and arm strength. Squeeze a sponge ball or a towel. Flex and extend the fingers and arms offering your own resistance to the movements. Plan a sensible exercise program that will increase your fitness for golf.

5. Address the ball and check the address position. As you do so "let go" especially through the shoulders so you will be relaxed and ready to move. Maintain a correct and firm grip.

6. Practice taking the stance to different targets. You can check to see if the stance is square by laying a club on the ground with the shaft touching the front tips of your shoes. Then step back of the ball and see if the club shaft is parallel with the intended line of flight. (fig. 4.13)

7. To register the feeling of the correct body posture in action, do this exercise. Without holding a club, assume an easy, comfortable stance. Check: feet—shoulder width apart, body bent forward from the hip joints, knees "easy," and arms hanging free of the body. Swing arms back and forth. Watch a spot on the ground to maintain a fairly steady head position. Let

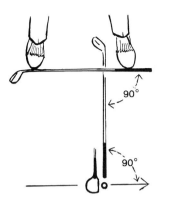

the body and legs "give" with the swing. Gradually increase the arm swing to a point where the shoulders alternately and naturally move under the chin. (fig. 9.2b) This is also a good warm-up exercise.

8. Make the steps in addressing the ball simple and concise. After you have had some practice in taking the stance avoid making a "production" of it. Place some trust in yourself to aim and to settle in a stance which is good for you.

Fig. 4.13 Checking alignment with golf clubs.

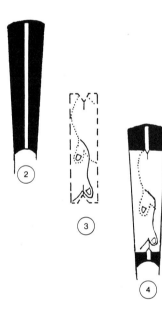

GRIP-GUIDE

How to Place GRIP-GUIDE Pattern on Club Handle

1. Set the sole of a medium iron flat on the ground, club-face pointing to the target.
2. Mark a line down the center front of the club-grip.
3. Follow outlining broken lines and cut out rectangular form of Grip-Guide. (Grip-Guide patterns are on page 25).

4. Place notches of Grip-Guide on center line of club handle and tape onto club.

How to Place Hands on Grip-Guide Pattern

The key to the correct hold on the club is placing the thumb and index finger of each hand on the pattern—top hand on dotted line and lower hand on solid line. With the positions of the thumbs and index fingers correct, the remaining fingers, as they are wrapped around the handle, will normally assume their proper positions.

1. *Top hand*—place thumb and index finger on dotted line and take hold of the club. Edge of index finger should fall on or near the dotted line indicated, forming a **V** between thumb and index finger.

Check-points for Top Hand:

a. Thumb slightly to side of center line.
b. **V** between thumb and index finger points in general direction of right shoulder. (Left-handers; left shoulder)
c. As you look down on the grip, the knuckles at base of first two fingers (and possibly third finger) can be seen.
d. Tip of thumb and lower edge of index finger are in a position approximately equidistant down the club handle.

2. *Lower hand*—place thumb and index finger in position on solid line. (Note **V** between thumb and edge of index finger). Wrap all fingers, except little finger, around handle. For the OVERLAPPING grip, let little finger overlap index finger of top hand; INTERLOCKING, interlock little finger and index finger of top hand; TEN-FINGER, wrap little finger with others around club.

Check-points for Lower Hand:

a. Thumb is slightly to side of center line.
b. **V** between thumb and index finger points in general direction of right shoulder. (Left-handers; left shoulder)
c. As you look down on the grip, the knuckle at base of index finger (and possibly long finger) can be seen.
d. Tip of thumb and lower edge of index finger are in a position approximately equidistant down the handle.
e. Palms of hands should face each other.

Adjustments

For extremely large or small hands, place the thumbs and index fingers in the same relative position that the Grip-Guide indicates, but outside or inside the guide lines. In most cases little or no adjustment will be necessary.

After placing the hands on the Grip-Guide in their proper positions, very slight adjustments may be made for greater ease in holding the club, but do not fail to keep thumb and index fingers close to pattern.

Safety Precautions

After Grip-Guide is taped firmly in place, practice taking the grip. When you feel you are holding the club securely and there is no danger of the club slipping out of your hands, practice taking the small swings and progress to the longer swings.

Grip-Guide should help you learn the correct grip. When you feel confident that you can hold the club properly, discontinue using the Guide. It has then served its purpose.

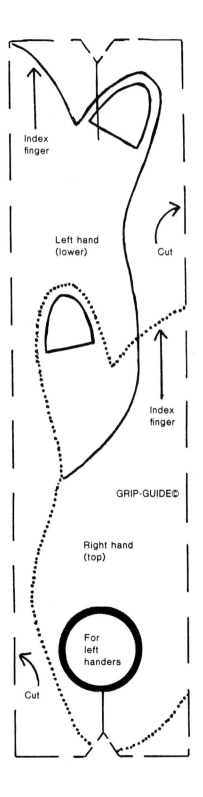

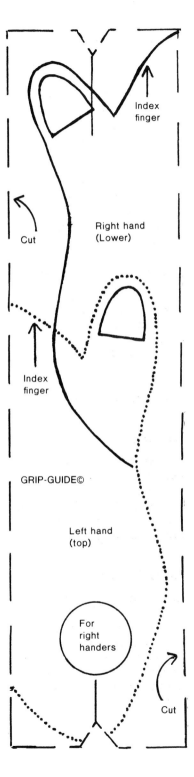

short approach shots

5

The short approach shots played to the putting green are *pitch shots* and *chip (or run-up) shots*. The pitch shot is played with a high lofted iron, thus the ball travels in a high trajectory and upon landing tends to stop with little or no forward roll. When a ball is contacted squarely with a lofted iron, the club face will compress the ball well below its center of gravity, thus imparting backspin to it. This backspin and the height from which the ball falls to the ground will tend to stop the forward motion of the ball when it lands. In some instances the ball will bounce backwards after landing.

The chip or run-up shot is usually stroked with a medium iron. The ball travels in a relatively low trajectory. The chip shot will, after landing, roll a longer distance than a typical pitch shot, due to the lack of backspin and to the low trajectory.

You do not need to learn two swings to hit the pitch and chip shots. The club-face loft—not the swing—produces the backspin and the trajectory of the ball. You have one swing to learn. Depending upon the desired distance, the swings will vary in length or circumference.

How does the flight and spin of the ball differ for chip and pitch shots? What factors determine your choice between these shots?

THE SWINGS

The swings for the short approach shots are relatively simple motions. The preliminary steps to taking the swings are defining your purpose and getting a clear picture in your mind of the action. Consider this situation:

Your ball is lying about five feet from the putting green and about forty-five feet from the hole. (fig. 5.5, ex. F) You choose to hit a run-up shot with a medium iron. The ball will travel in the air a short distance, land on the green, and then roll toward the target—the hole.

Fig. 5.1   Approximate one-quarter swing

Picture the swing as a pendulum motion with the clubhead swinging in a shallow arc—away from the ball and then through the ball toward your target.

Check your grip and stance. For more clubhead control, grip down ("choke up") on the club-handle. Practice swinging without using a ball. Direct your attention to these cues:

1. Swing the clubhead low and close to the ground. Sweep the grass with the clubhead—at the beginning of the backswing and on the forward swing through the impact area.
2. Keep the swing even and smooth. Feel that both hands are working together. In your early trials you may note that the swing varies. You will not cut or sweep the same grass in each swing. This is normal. With practice you will gain a sense of control with the hands. You will develop a "touch" for swinging the clubhead—the swing will "groove" itself.

After you gain some control in swinging the club, try striking the ball to your target. Make no extra effort to "hit" the ball or loft it into the air.

You will no doubt hit balls beyond and short of your target. You will decrease or increase the length of your swing to hit the ball the desired distance. You will be registering in your "muscle memory" how far you must swing the clubhead to stroke the ball different distances.

Fig. 5.2   Half swing

As the distance to the hole increases, besides swinging the club in a longer arc, you may take a wider stance and move your hands up on the club handle. Some additional cues for stroking the ball longer distances are:

1. Do not try to "hit harder" or speed up the clubhead. The larger arc produces greater clubhead speed. Keep the same tempo in swinging the hands as you had in the smaller swings.
2. Be sensitive in your fingers and hands to swinging and gaining control of the clubhead.
3. Watch the club-face strike the ball. Do not be over-anxious to see the shot result.

The terms *one-quarter*, *one-half*, and *three-quarter* are often used to describe the approximate length of approach swings. You learn through practice and experience how far to swing the club for a given distance. You sight and judge the distance for a shot, and then through the remarkable sense of "feel," or kinesthetic sense, you swing the club the distance your eye, "feel," and experience indicate. There is a subconscious translation of this synthesis of judgments into the execution of the golf shot. At times all golfers experience the thrill of executing approach shots expertly—either by having the ball come to rest inches from the hole or by holing out the approach shot. (The three-quarter swing is discussed in chapter 6.)

STROKE EXECUTION—SOME ANALYSIS AND DETAIL

You need not concentrate on numerous details to develop the swing. The details of the motion may be the result of having the correct grip and stance, and swinging the clubhead with the correct purpose in mind.

1. The clubhead is swung in an arc, keeping the same radius throughout the swing. *Result*—the left arm will maintain the easy extended position it assumed in addressing the ball.
2. During the swing there is a lack of tension in the shoulders and arms. *Result*—there is a free arm and shoulder motion in the swing.
3. The grip is correct and firm but not tense. *Result*—there will be a gradual bending of the wrists if the clubhead is swung. If the handle of the club is carried back and forth or if it is lifted, there can be no normal responsive action of the wrists. The cooperative action of the wrists becomes more apparent as the swing lengthens. Wrist action is a very gradual motion. It does not occur at a certain spot in the swing. There is no conscious effort to "use" the wrists.
4. As the swing begins the stance is comfortable and there is a slight bend of the knees. *Result*—there may be a slight give of the body towards the direction of the swing—but not a "give" of the head. As you swing back the left knee will naturally give to the right side, and there will be a tendency for a slight weight shift to the right foot. As you swing through, the opposite action occurs. Like the wrist motion, this action of the body and legs becomes greater and more evident as the swing lengthens.

There is a fusion of all details into a unit of motion. Good form can develop as a result of swinging the clubhead.

Grip, Hand Action, and Wrist Action

If the grip is changed during the swing, an awkward action in the hands and wrists is almost certain to occur. You can check your swing at any point to see if your grip has remained correct. The check is exactly the same as the one used in the address position. Stop your swing at the point where you wish to check it, move your head so that you are looking at your grip, just as you did in the address position, and apply the check points to the grip. In this checking do not move your head until you stop the swing. Suppose you wish to check your grip at the end of the backswing. Take the correct grip, address the ball properly, and swing the club back and stop. Hold this position. Turn your head to the side so it is in the same *relative position* to your hands as at the address. Now check the grip. The grip should be the same as at the address.

A common fault in making the swing for the short approach shot is attempting to scoop the ball up into the air. In this erroneous action the hands, instead of working together, work in opposition to each other. Near ball impact the right hand moves forward and under, as the left hand holds back. A common outcome of this error is striking the ground with the club-head before striking the ball. Through the impact area both hands must move with the clubhead. At times there may be a feeling that the hands are leading the clubhead. (See Ch. 9, fig. 9.4)

You can easily check and rehearse the wrist action that occurs in the swing. Keeping the arms extended as in the address position, raise the club-head and point it forward and then over your right shoulder. When you point the clubhead over your right shoulder, keep the left elbow easily ex-tended and let the right elbow bend. Note that if you lift the clubhandle with the arms there will be no bending of the wrists. (fig. 5.3)

Knee Action and Foot Action

Action of the knees, feet, and legs is a part of swinging the clubhead in a certain direction. Because of previously developed muscle habits and tension there might be a lack of response in developing this combined action. Rather than complicating the swing by thinking of how to move your feet or which foot to move, this part of the swing can be practiced by itself without break-ing up the blending action of all parts of the swing. A simple practice exercise is to alternate bending the left knee toward a spot in front of the right foot, and then bending the right knee so that it points to a spot in front of the left foot. Accompanying this knee bending is some inward action of the ankle and foot. The weight shifts to the inner border of the foot and big toe. The heel may rise slightly from the ground with the inner border rising less than the

Fig. 5.3   Wrist action exercise

Fig. 5.4   Foot and leg action exercise

outer border. When you have trained your muscles to move in this manner and have developed a "feeling" for the motion, then you can expect to move the legs and feet correctly when you swing the club. This practice exercise plus the directional influence of the swing will help develop a correct and natural action. (fig. 5.4)

Head Position

In all golf swings the head remains in a fairly stationary position until after the ball is struck. After ball contact, your head will turn naturally to accommodate the follow-through of the swing. There should be no question about this correct mechanical aspect of the swing. The cue "watch the ball until you strike it" accomplishes the steady head position for most people. The cue "keep your head down" can result in serious errors if the idea is overemphasized. If one were to keep his head down so that his chin is resting on his chest, it would be impossible to make a good golf swing. As the body turns during the swing the shoulder moves under the chin. The "head down" position tends to block what should be the natural movement of the shoulders and body. One other serious error that may result from exaggerating this cue is moving the head down and lower during the backswing. This binds the backswing. Then, because the head must be moved back up into the address position when the ball is struck, the control and the momentum of the club-head are destroyed. Until after impact your head should remain fairly still and in the position it is in at the address. However, you should not hold yourself rigid; neither should you concentrate solely on the position of your head.

APPROACH SITUATIONS AND CLUB SELECTION

In certain approach situations there is little or no choice in the shot you must play. In situation A, figure 5.5, you must hit over a deep bunker, land the ball on the green, and have it stay there . . . use a high lofted iron and hit a pitch shot. In situation B, you must strike the ball so it will travel low under the limbs of a tree . . . use an iron with little loft and play a chip shot. In situation C, figure 5.6, the area of green to which you must play the ball is small and the green slopes downhill . . . hit a run-up shot into the bank of the hill so that the ball will bounce off the bank onto the green.

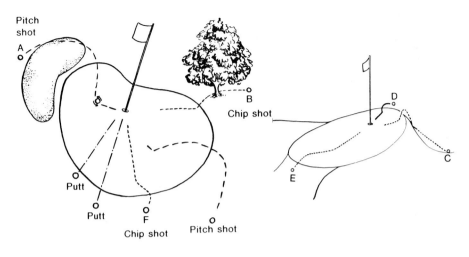

Fig. 5.5   Fig. 5.6

When there is a choice in the shot you can play, consider:

1. *Your skill.* Use the club in which you have confidence and success. When practical to do so, choose the chip shot over the pitch shot. First, it is an easier shot for most golfers. Second, if an error such as topping or half-topping is made, the error in shot result is likely to be less with the chip shot. For a given distance a pitch shot must be struck with greater force than a chip shot. Thus, in the pitch shot if the ball is erroneously hit above center, it is likely to roll far past the hole and putting green.

2. *The condition of the course.* If the putting green is dried out and hard, pitch shots will not "hold" on the green. Use run-up shots under these conditions. Ordinarily, do not use chip shots when the ground is very wet and soft.

3. *The contour of the green and the position of the cup.* Allow for the ball to roll more when it lands on a downhill surface and to roll less when it lands on an uphill surface. In situation D, fig. 5.6, the surface is downhill and the hole is close to the edge of the green. Usually an iron with loft would be used to counteract the tendency of the ball to roll downhill. In situation E, a medium iron would be used for a run-up shot. The putting stroke may be your most effective approach when a lofted shot is not needed and when the ball will roll easily on the grass (fig. 5.5 and 5.6). In situations D and E (fig. 5.6), most golfers will consider using either an approach iron or a putter. The decision will be based on their experience in playing the stroke and on the situation, which includes the condition of the turf around the green.

4. *The lie of the ball.* If the ball is lying on thin turf or on bare ground, it usually is easier to stroke the ball effectively with a medium iron than with a high lofted iron.

PRACTICE SUGGESTIONS

1. Review some basics of the Grip, Stance and Swing

   Grip

   a. Hold the club, do not grip it tightly. Relax the forearms, arms, and shoulders. Grip down on the handle for short distance shots.
   b. Check the grip: Palms face each other with the right palm facing the target. The V's formed by the thumbs and index fingers point in the general direction of the right shoulder. The left thumb fits in the life-line of the right palm.

   Stance

   a. Place club-sole flat on ground with the club-face pointing to the target, then move feet into a narrow stance. Clubhead is in a position approximately out from the center of the stance.
   b. The left arm and club-shaft are in approximately a straight line. Hands may be slightly ahead of clubhead.
   c. Assume a comfortable, balanced stance with the knees slightly bent.

   Swing

   a. Define the target. For chip shots use a medium iron; for pitch shots use a high-lofted iron. Visualize the ball travelling to the target. Rehearse a "feeling" of the swing.
   b. Concentrate on swinging the clubhead—away from your target and toward it. Do not "tie yourself up" by thinking of details.
   c. Let the tool—clubhead—work for you. Swing the clubhead low through the impact area.

2. Picture the action of a playground swing—swinging back-and-forth, back-and-forth. Swing the clubhead in this rhythmic manner. Sweep the grass with each back-and-forth motion. The clubhead speed will be the same for the backswing and the forward swing.

   You will note how the continuous motion creates certain details of good form. The wrists "give" or bend, acting as hinges, allowing the clubhead to swing in a longer arc than the hands. Due to the outward pull of the swing (centrifugal force) the left arm swings in an extended position. The body and legs give in the direction of the swing.

   Without striking a ball, practice one swing at a time. Watch the clubhead sweep the grass at the start of the swing and through the impact area. *Hold* the finish of the swing and feel control of the club with the hands.

3. Hit many chip shots from near the green. Practice until you are machine-like in performance so that there need be no thought regarding how to execute the shot. Aim to roll the ball into the cup, and if the ball does not drop into the cup, have it come to rest very close to the hole. You may find it helpful to pick out a spot on the green where you wish to have the ball land.

SHARON MILLER, Member Advisory Staff, Ping Golf Clubs
(Karsten Mfg. Corp.)

4. Work from short approaches to longer ones. Change your target both for distance and line of direction. Learn to aim and judge distance. Make mental notes on the different length shots, i.e., how much to "choke up" on the grip; the width of the stance; the necessary length of swing.
5. Practice stroking the ball from good lies on the turf. When you increase your skill, try stroking the ball from good and poor lies. Stroking the ball from other than a good lie is not so much a matter of learning how to do it but rather a matter of facing the situation without anxiety. Practice from various lies, but do not continue practice from poor lies if you are not having success. Such practice tends to destroy confidence and disrupt a good swing pattern.
6. Practice both chip shots and pitch shots. In changing from hitting chip shots to hitting pitch shots, you may "feel" a difference in the swings. For example: you are hitting chip shots 30 yards with a 5-iron, you then change to a 9-iron or wedge to pitch the same distance. When you use the higher lofted iron for the pitch shot, it will be necessary to take a longer swing. You have already noted that there is more responsive wrist action as the swing lengthens, so naturally you might sense more wrist action in the pitch shot. The longer swing and the differences in club-

BETH STONE, Member, Advisory Staff, Ben Hogan Golf Co.

head weights and shaft lengths all contribute to what you sense about the stroke. This is a result—to purposely try to develop two different swings for the chip shot and the pitch shot is neither necessary nor recommended. Postpone practice with the wedge until you have developed some real skill with the other short irons.

7. In your practice take a comfortable stance. You may prefer a slightly open stance, but do not adopt one which is not "easy" for you. You must be in balance and comfortable to hit these delicate shots. It is possible to change the ball flight by changing the position from which you play the ball. If you play the ball from a point more nearly opposite the right side of the stance, the ball will tend to travel in a low trajectory; a ball struck from a point more nearly opposite the left side of the stance will tend to travel in a high trajectory. After you have developed skill in swinging and in stroking the ball, this information on changing ball flight trajectory can be useful to you.

8. These exercises will help you develop a feeling of swinging the clubhead and sensing control in the fingers and hands.

PAT BRADLEY, Member, Advisory Staff, Ram Golf Corp.

   a. Reverse the club and grip the shaft near the clubhead so the end of the handle is about 6 inches from the ground. Swing the tip of the handle in the air back and forth continuously. Then reverse the club and take your regular grip on the handle and swing the clubhead. After continuous swinging practice, follow the same procedure of reversing the club, but take one swing at a time. You will definitely feel the clubhead after swinging the comparatively weightless handle.

   b. Practice swinging as in (a) above, but with your eyes closed. You will note even greater sensitivity of clubhead control in the fingers and hands and of feeling the whole swing.

  9. Practice swinging in front of a mirror. Pay particular attention to the clubhead arc.

10. Stand with your feet together and take an approximate one-half swing. This stance will require you to swing in balance. You may be surprised at how well and how far you can hit a ball while standing in this position.

   Short strokes are an important part of your game. Spend the first part of every practice session on them.

the full strokes—
irons and woods
6

Essentially, there is no difference in the way you swing the wood club and the full iron. The swings may feel different to you. This is reasonable, for there are differences in shaft lengths, club balances, club weights, the speeds of the swings, and the arcs of the swings. In the wood swing the path of the clubhead is closer and more level to the ground for a longer distance through the contact area than it is with the irons. The wood swing may feel more like a sweep than the swing with the irons. One often hears that in playing an iron there should be a feeling of hitting down on the ball. If exaggerated, this cue can lead to trouble. The swing through the contact area, for both woods and irons, should be one of hitting the ball toward a distant target. The experienced golfer can try hitting down and because of his experience in handling a club, he may not encounter difficulty. For the novice who is trying to learn the swing, this idea of "hitting down" may result in a poor swing and a poor shot. The best idea for most players is to *hit the ball out toward the target*. The swing may feel downward, but do not try to force such an action.

THE SWINGS

Playing the High Lofted Irons

When you use the high lofted irons, #7 and above, you have a short club designed for a high degree of accuracy. A swing somewhat less than the full swing is recommended for these shots. This is sensible for there is less movement involved in a three-quarter swing than in a full swing, thus a greater chance of being accurate. This motion is an extension of the half swing. No great effort need be made to increase the swing. With a purpose of stroking the ball a slightly ·longer distance, you will naturally take a longer swing. Some fine players use an approximate three-quarter swing (fig. 6.1) for all the full iron shots and for the wood shots.

Fig. 6.1   Approximate three-quarter swing

As you read the analysis of the full swing, you will find several references to rhythm and tempo. Give at least three points to remember about these elements of the swing.

A Look at the Full Swing and Some Analysis

Addressing the Ball (for complete review, see Ch. 4)

1. Aim to a definite target within your distance potential.
2. Take a comfortable balanced stance—feet approximately shoulder width apart. The stance may be slightly narrower for the irons.
3. Arms should hang easily from the shoulders. The left arm and club shaft are in approximately a straight line.
4. If a waggle of the club is made—make it a rehearsal for the start of the backswing—keep the clubhead low as it is moved back away from the ball.

Starting the Swing

1. The feeling of starting the clubhead away from the ball should be one of ease. Do not hurry as you begin the swing. Do not lift or grab the club handle.

2. The clubhead is swung back close to the ground. The hands, arms, and shoulders move as a unit accompanied by a natural "give" of the legs and body.

3. The feeling and effort is one of swinging the clubhead straight back away from the ball, but after a certain point the clubhead will normally swing inside the intended line of ball flight. Half-way into the backswing, the hands, easily extended arms, and the clubhead will be approximately opposite the right side.

Fig. 6.2   Addressing the ball.

Fig. 6.3   Starting the backswing.

Fig. 6.4   Top of the swing

Fig. 6.5   Top of the swing—side view

Top of the Swing

1. The club shaft is approximately horizontal.
2. The left arm is easily extended in order to maintain the swing radius. The right elbow is bent and pointing down, comfortably and slightly away from the side. (Avoid trying to keep the right elbow against the right side. Such action binds the swing and reduces the radius of the arc).
3. The wrists are bent (cocked) and in a position approximately under the club handle. The correct grip has been maintained.
4. The body has turned (shoulders and hips) so the left shoulder is under the chin. To accommodate this coiling of the body, some weight has shifted to the right side and the left leg has responded in the direction of the swing. (Avoid trying to keep the left heel flat on the ground. This restriction usually inhibits a free body turn and for some people may cause back strain).
5. The arc of the swing is naturally and simultaneously around the body and upward.

Downswing

1. The swing should feel like one complete motion even though there is a change of direction. Avoid any tendency to rush into the downswing. When the start of the downswing "feels" slow, it is likely to be correct. Let the clubhead speed develop later in the downswing.

Fig. 6.6   Downswing

Fig. 6.7   Downswing—side view

2. The downswing is a blended gathering of forces for contacting the ball with a swiftly moving clubhead. As a result:
    a. The left heel returns to its original position on the ground and the body weight begins to shift to the left side.
    b. The arms swing downward with the left arm remaining in its extended position, and the right elbow coming into the right side.
    c. The wrists remain in a cocked position reserving clubhead acceleration for a split second later.
    d. The hips shift slightly to the left and the body starts to turn in the direction of the swing.
These actions merge one into the other.

Impact

1. The body is in a firm position of balance to allow the clubhead to reach its optimum speed at ball contact. The clubhead catches up with the hands. The hands, arms, and clubhead move through the impact area together. (Avoid trying to hold the hands and arms back while trying to "snap" the wrists and clubhead).
2. The head remains fairly still. "Watch the club-face strike the ball" is a useful cue.

Follow-Through

1. Through the impact area the clubhead swings close to the ground and on the intended line of ball flight, and then gradually moves inside that line and upward.
2. The objective, hitting the ball to a distant target, along with the swiftly moving clubhead produces a follow-through in good form.

Fig. 6.8   Impact   Fig. 6.9

Fig. 6.10   Follow-through

3. At the finish of the swing the shoulders and hips have turned so the body is facing the intended target. The head has turned (not raised up) to accommodate the full finish and to see the shot result. The right knee has bent and turned so it is touching (or near) the left knee. The right heel is well off the ground. The body is in good balance with most of the weight shifted to the left foot.

THE SEARCH FOR DISTANCE—CAUTIONS AND SUGGESTIONS

Progressing to the point of stroking the ball with the long irons and woods should not be a complicated step. Your objective is to strike the ball to a more distant target, but a target within your distance potential. If the objective should become hitting the ball with all one's might, complications arise: poor coordinations, muscle tensions, and poor timing. They are the curse of the beginner and experienced player alike.

Muscular Contraction and Relaxation

Some practical knowledge about muscle action can be helpful. Try this experiment related to using muscles effectively and ineffectively. Extend your right arm out in front of you with your palm facing up. Bend the right elbow and touch your fingers to your shoulder. Return the arm to your side. Now extend your arm out similarly again but this time tightly tense, (contract) all the muscles of your arm. Keeping your muscles tense, try bending your elbow. This action is now difficult, if not impossible. Why? You are preventing muscles used in the motion to perform. When you relax—let go— they can perform. Tensing up when you want the arm to move is like stepping on your car's accelerator and brake at the same time.

If you try to hit the ball "hard," as far as or even farther than you can, you tend to use muscles in such a way that they resist and even "block" the intended movement. This great exertion involved in tensing up the muscles gives you the *false feeling* that this is the way to accomplish the goal of hitting the ball a long distance.

Muscular contractions of resistance plus the strong muscular contractions to overcome the resistance may make you feel more powerful, but they spell ruin for distance and accuracy of a golf stroke. As a novice or an experienced player, you can be easily misled by the "feeling" of a golf swing. When you hit a fine shot a considerable distance you are apt to think or say: "I swung so easy." That is true. You did swing easy "musclewise." The muscle action was synchronized. Resistant muscular contractions were avoided, and the right muscular contractions were made so the swing felt "good." After such an experience you may think: "If I can hit the ball that far swinging 'easy,' then I'll put something into the swing and really hit the ball farther." This theorizing may seem logical. But what will you put into the swing? If it is more clubhead speed, then you can expect a longer shot. If you are misled by the feeling of "muscling the ball," then you probably can expect to hit the ball a shorter distance. When the swing felt "easy," and possibly slow, you may have been swinging with the greatest clubhead speed.

Timing the Swing

If you can avoid "hurrying to hit" the ball, your chances for developing and maintaining well-timed swings are good. Speeding up the swing to hit the ball great distances destroys tempo and rhythm and produces poor and painful golf shots—so much is put into the motion and so little is gained. A well-timed swing produces accuracy and optimum speed at and through ball contact. Consider these suggestions to help you time your swing.

1. Since the swing is started from a still position, it must begin slowly and evenly. Then a gradual and smooth acceleration of the clubhead follows.
2. The feet, legs, body, arms, and hands must work together, each supplying its own power. Arguing and trying to reach a decision on whether a particular body part plays a more important role in timing or in power is futile. The fact that you can move your hands and arms faster than you can move your body and legs furnishes a lead for timing. You cannot "flail away" with the hands and arms and have the legs and body trying to "catch up" by lunging and jerking. The arms and hands must be attuned to the speed at which the legs and body can move.
3. Many players find that counting helps their swings. The backswing is counted as 1, the top of the swing 2, and the downswing 3; or, 1 - and - 2; or, back - and - through. Some players use only two counts; some use key words which have significance for them.
4. Keeping the same tempo and rhythm for all strokes is recommended. Key your timing to a medium iron and maintain the same tempo when you progress to the long irons and woods. Many a player has ruined a golf game by keying his timing to fast swings with the driver. A player rushes

to the golf course, takes a few strenuous swings with the driver and hits a few practice shots as hard as he can. During the round this player is likely to say: "My timing is off today."

The synchronization of a fine golf swing that produces accurate and long golf shots is beyond human description, but within human achievement.

DISTANCES AND CLUB SELECTION

The Irons

You will learn through practice how far you can hit with each iron. Until you gain some experience there probably will be little difference in the distance you can stroke the ball with the various clubs. You may get greater distance with the medium irons than you do with the long irons. This should not concern you. After hitting many practice shots, you will learn to time your swing correctly for the different lengths of clubs, thus hitting the ball the optimum distance with each club.

The irons are versatile clubs. You can hit the ball from various situations with them. You can make certain adjustments to vary the distances and trajectories of ball flight. For instance, the distance you wish to hit the ball requires a full 6-iron shot. You have only a #5 and a #7-iron. Do not try to extend the distance you normally can hit with the 7-iron. Take a 5-iron, either grip down on the handle or take a shorter swing or do both. Keep the same tempo in the swing as you would in making any golf stroke. Do not purposely slow down the swing.

If, with any specific iron, you wish to hit the ball in a higher or lower trajectory than normal for that club, you change the angle of the club face when you address the ball. Increasing the club face angle to get more loft to the shot is called "opening the face," and decreasing the angle is called "closing the face."

The Woods

When you play golf on a regulation course you probably will tee off with a wood on at least fourteen of the eighteen holes. (Most courses have four par-3 holes, and all or some of these holes may be less than wood length distance). The driver is designed to hit the ball from a tee. Only in rare circumstances would it be used from the fairway.

On many of the long holes your drive from the tee will be followed by using a wood if the lie of the ball and the distance warrant it. The lie of the ball is more important than the distance in deciding whether you will use a wood and what wood you will use. The higher lofted woods, #4, #5, and above can be used for poorer lies and shorter distances than the #3 wood. Even though you are a wood distance from the green, the circumstances under which you must play the ball may necessitate your using an iron rather than a wood.

Based on your ability, what club would you use for teeing off on par 3 holes with distances of: 90, 105, 130, and 170 yds.?

PRACTICE SUGGESTIONS

1. Take short and full swings without hitting a ball. Work for a smooth swing. Watch the clubhead cut the grass through the impact area. If you wish to check the position of your head, stand so your shadow casts in front of you. Do exercises to develop the correct footwork and body turn. (fig. 6.11, 6.12)

2. Swing the club as if it were a baseball bat. Take the golf grip and let the left arm remain easily extended during the swing. First, swing at an imaginary ball shoulder height, then about waist height, then lower, until you are swinging at one on the ground.
   On every swing, first swing the club over your right shoulder and then over your left shoulder.

3. After you feel you are swinging the club with control, take both short and full practice swings, holding the club with the left hand only. This practice may help strengthen your left arm and give you a feeling of left hand control.

4. If you are stroking the ball from artificial turf or from hard ground, do not try to hit down and take divots with iron shots. The reverberation of the shock of hitting a hard surface could injure the hands, wrists, or arms. A divot may be the result of a good shot, but taking a divot is not a "must" for hitting good iron shots. Many fine iron shots are hit without taking a divot.

Fig. 6.11

Fig. 6.12

LEE TREVINO, Pictures by Irv Schloss. Courtesy of Faultless Golf Products, Division of Abbott Laboratories.

SAM SNEAD, Courtesy of Wilson Sporting Goods Co.

5. Work from the short iron shots to the full shots with the irons and woods. Do not start practice by trying to hit long shots with a driver: there is a chance of muscle and joint strain without a warm-up; and too much emphasis is placed on "hitting hard" rather than on developing and "grooving" a good swing.

6. If the long iron and wood shots are unsatisfactory, try gripping down on the club-handle. This shorter hold on the club may give you better control and more successful shots. Gradually work up to the full hold on the club.

7. If you are having trouble hitting shots off the grass—irons and woods— place the ball on a tee. After you have some success in hitting the ball from a tee, return to hitting shots from good positions on the grass. Do not have any misgivings about hitting fairway woods and irons from a tee and from good lies on the grass. Successful shots can restore your confidence so you can stroke the ball from any position.

8. Choose a specific target for each shot. Learn how far you can hit the ball with each club. Learn to hit the ball 75, 100, 130 yards, etc. This practice will prepare you for playing golf.

GENE LITTLER, Courtesy Ram Golf Corporation

the putting stroke

7

If open putting tournaments were held—to include men and women, amateurs and professionals—it would be unwise to bet only on the professionals to win. Many average golfers are exceptionally skillful in putting.

The putting stroke allows you to assert your individuality. You can choose a putter from perhaps a hundred or more differing styles. Some players use the same club throughout their golfing years. At the other extreme are the golfers who blame the club for all their golfing woes. They change putters frequently—always in search of a "magic" putter. Ways of holding the club and taking the stance differ. Just as there is no best club,

---

Line up 6 balls around the cup on the practice putting green, starting at 2 feet from the hole. Putt all 6 balls into the cup, rolling them right into the center of the hole. Move back to a distance of 4 feet from the hole and attempt to sink the putts from there. Continue the same practice for longer putts.

1. Check your position addressing the ball. Are you relaxed and comfortable? Is the sole of the putter flat on the ground? Are your eyes directly above the ball? Do you have the ball lined up with the center of the club face?

2. Check your stroke. Does the putter head stay close to the ground? Are you swinging the putter approximately on the correct line? Is the stroke smooth and easy?

3. Test your progress and accuracy in putting. Are the 1- to 2-foot putts becoming almost automatic to make? Are you able to sink a greater number of long putts than formerly? When you miss a putt, does the ball come to rest very close to the hole so that the next putt is an easy "tap in."

there is no best way to hold the putter and stand at the ball. Expert putters, however, agree on and follow certain basics. They do not stray too far from widely accepted principles.

ADDRESSING THE BALL

If you can address the ball with a quiet confidence your chances of putting well are enhanced. Be comfortable and easy in both your grip and stance.

The Hold on the Club

The most widely used grip is the reverse-overlapping grip in which the left index finger overlaps the little finger of the right hand. Or, an alternative is to extend the left index finger down overlapping more than one finger of the right hand. (fig. 7.1) The thumbs are straight down the front of shaft with the palms facing each other. You may either hold the club at its full length or "choke up" on the grip slightly. Hold the club with a gentle firmness.

The Stance

Narrow, medium, or wide—square, open, or closed—all are acceptable. Whatever stance you choose, make it a balanced and comfortable one.

Place the sole of the putter flat on the putting surface back of the ball with the club-face pointing to the target. This position results in your standing close to the ball, with the arms close to the body and the elbows bent. Your head is in a position directly above the ball so you are looking straight down on it. The knees are bent and "easy."

Play the ball in a position similar to other golf shots—from a point opposite the left foot to a point opposite the center of the stance. If the ball is played at the extreme left of the stance, more of your weight may be carried on the left foot.

Fig. 7.1   Reverse-overlapping grip

Back View   Front View

Fig. 7.2   Putting stance

THE SWING

Swing the putter-head back and through close to the ground in a pendulum-like motion. The length of the swing will vary with the distance of the putt. For short distances swing the clubhead back and through on the intended line of roll. On long putts your feeling may be one of swinging the putter on the line, but as the swing increases in length the putter-head will naturally swing inside the intended line of roll on the backswing and follow-through.

Your purpose—stroking (not hitting) the ball so it will roll across the carpet-like grass into the hole—should create this simple swing. The subtle combined movement of the hands, wrists, and arms will blend into one whole smooth swing. Don't dismantle this stroke with analysis! Swing the clubhead in a pendulum-like manner to roll the ball into the hole.

The body remains still. It has no contribution to make to this small swing, except to provide stability.

As in all golf strokes, watch the club-face stroke the ball. Ease is a key to good putting.

AIMING

To aim, simply have the face of the club pointing to your objective. Your objective may be the hole or a spot on the green if you have to allow for a sidehill roll of the ball. When you address the ball, be certain it is lined up with the center of the club-face, never toward the toe of the club. It may be helpful to momentarily place the putter head in front of the ball to line up the face with the target. In the address position turn your head to the target while you sight and visualize the desired putt, then run your eyes back along the line to the ball. Proceed to stroke the ball without delay. Delay induces tension.

Your goal should be to roll the ball into the cup. If the ball does not drop into the hole then you want it to come to rest inches or less from the hole. The adage "never up, never in" is a good one to remember. Putt the ball as far as the hole. Only then does it have a chance to drop in the cup.

JUDGMENT FACTORS

In addition to judging distances, you have other judgments to make. You must figure how to play a slope or undulation. You must learn to judge how easily the ball will roll over the putting surface. This is called "reading" a green. As you wait your turn to putt, try to stand near your ball, preferably behind it. (See rules of etiquette.) When your turn comes to putt, you have already studied your line and figured any "break" (contour) of the green. As you wait, also learn from watching other putts. If you have a sidehill putt, and another player has already played a similar stroke, then you have the best information you can get for playing your putt.

Putting greens are referred to as "fast" or "slow," depending upon how easily the ball rolls over the surface. The condition and type of grass determines how fast or slow a green will be. If the turf is thin and dried out the green will be faster than if the turf is thick and wet. Various grasses are used for putting greens. One type—a bent grass—affects the roll of the ball. A putt against the grain requires a firmer stroke and a putt with the grain a lighter stroke. You can make some judgment as to how fast or how slow greens will be by practicing on the practice green before you start your round. You can also watch the stroke results of your companions during play.

What is meant by these expressions: reading the green, hitting the green, shooting for a birdie, and rimming the cup?

PUTTING—THE KEY TO LOW SCORES

The top tournament professional golfers, men and women, shoot sub-par rounds often. The key stroke in their below-par rounds is putting. If a professional golfer were asked: "Of all the golf strokes, which one would you want at its peak during a tournament?" The answer would be unanimous: "Putting."

If par is 72 for a course, 36 strokes are allotted to reach the putting green and 36 strokes are assigned for putting. In a round of 18 holes, all players— from the novice to the professional—can often expect to take less than 36 putts, but rarely can players expect to take less than 36 strokes to reach the putting greens. Reaching a green in the par figure allotted for a hole is commonly called either "being on in regulation" or "hitting the green." If you read that a professional player was "on in regulation" on all 18 holes or that he "hit 18 greens" you will know that he was on the putting green in the distance allotment figures on all 18 holes. When this golfer plays his first putt on each green, he is shooting for a score of 1 under par for the hole—a *birdie*. If he takes 1 putt on 6 of the greens and 2 putts on the other 12 greens, thereby taking a total of 30 putts and scoring six birdies and twelve pars, his score for the par 72 course will be 66—a superb round of golf! Taking less than 36 putts and reaching the greens in near regulation figures is the way sub-par rounds are customarily made.

It would be most unusual for a player to take 36 putts and score below par for a round, because there are few greens, if any, that a player can reach in less than regulation figures. Par 5 holes for men and par 5 and par 6 holes for women can sometimes be reached in less than regulation by long hitters. If a player reaches the green of a par 5 hole in two shots or reaches the green of a par 6 hole in three shots, he or she is then putting for a score of 2 under par for the hole—an *eagle*. It is possible, but rare, for a player to reach the green of a par 4 hole in one stroke. The hole must be either especially short for its par or unusual conditions must exist, such as, hard ground or wind aiding the distance of the shot from the tee.

Putting gives you chances to score under par on certain holes and opportunities to make up for any error shots in your play from the tee to the putting green. *You cannot become a good player until you become a consistently good putter.*

Why is putting the key to below par scores?

PRACTICE SUGGESTIONS

1. Use several golf balls and start your practice with the balls about a foot away from the hole. Simply stroke the balls into the cup with little or no thought on "how" to putt. Gradually increase the distance. Let your "instinct" for aiming and judging take over. If the ball does not fall into the cup, it should come to rest very close to the hole.

2. Stroke the ball and listen for it to drop in the cup. This will help train you to remain calm and confident, not anxious about the result. The person who starts steering a putt immediately upon contacting the ball expects to miss the putt, not make it.

3. Practice at home on carpeting. It does not matter if the surface is different from grass. You are practicing to develop a stroke and swing.

4. When necessary, review some putting fundamentals. Then proceed to concentrate on sinking putts.

5. After a session of starting with short putts and working back to long distances, try a variety of putts—short, long, uphill, downhill, sidehill, and from off the apron of the green. Practice lining up the putts without delay. Learn to size up the situation and proceed at once to make the putt.

BILLY CASPER, Courtesy of Wilson Sporting Goods Co.

6. If in practice or play the putts are "rimming" the cup, with many close putts and "just misses," do not fret. You are putting well. The putts will start dropping so do not change this good stroke.

7. On sidehill putts visualize the curved path on which the ball must roll to drop into the cup. Pick out a spot on this path for your point of aim— as a bowler might do in spot bowling. Use such points as a different colored section of grass or a dead blade of grass. (A dead blade of grass may be removed, but if it is an aid in aiming, make use of it. It will not deflect the roll of the ball.)

8. Stroke the ball so it will roll smoothly over the green. The ball should not bob up and down—it should "hug" the putting surface in a forward end-over-end roll—*overspin*. You can easily check the roll of the ball: draw a circumference line around the ball with a colored marking pencil, place the ball in a position so the marked line is in the vertical plane, and then stroke the ball and check to see if the line stays in the same plane.

9. For self-testing practice, play nine different holes of a putting course. Par would be 18 for the nine holes. Check the number of strokes you are above or below par. Some of your practice may be in match or stroke competition with another player. This practice is enjoyable, stimulating, and challenging.

10. A practice session should last at least twenty minutes. After you have had some experience in putting avoid analysis and details of action. Work on a smooth, easy, and comfortable stroke. Anyone who can swing a putter can learn to putt well. Good putting is up to you!

shots requiring special consideration

8

PLAYING FROM A BUNKER (SAND TRAP)

To make golf more interesting and challenging, shallow to deep depressions filled with sand are placed strategically on the course. The USGA calls these areas bunkers; most people, however, refer to them as sand traps. In bunkers, creeks, and lakes (hazards), you may *not* touch the surface of the area before taking your forward swing to hit the ball—you may *not ground* the club. You may take a practice swing provided you do not touch the surface of the hazard. (See Ch. 10, Rules)

You may decide the best way to play a shot from a bunker by checking: (1) the lie of the ball; (2) the physical features of the hazard and the area beyond it; and (3) the desired distance of the shot. From a shallow bunker with the ball lying in a good position on the sand, few, if any, adjustments need be made. But if the bunker is a deep pit with overhanging turf, or if the ball is partially buried in the sand, you will have to play your shot differently than the ordinary golf stroke. Here are some typical situations you may encounter.

1. *Your ball is in a shallow trap 225 yards from the green. The ball is lying in a good position on the sand.*

   Plan on hitting the ball out of the trap to a position where you can hit the next shot onto the green. (Only the highly-skilled can reach the green from this distance and in this situation)

   Use a club in which you have confidence. Work your feet well down into the sand to attain a firm stance and thus maintain your balance. Swing smoothly—not violently—with the idea of stroking the ball to your target. Try to contact the ball before you contact any sand. If the ball is lying well up on the sand, you may hit the ball cleanly so the sand is scarcely disturbed by the clubhead.

a.   b.

c.   d.

Fig. 8.1   "Explosion" shot from sand trap (Michael Hemphill).

2. Your ball is lying in a shallow trap adjacent to the green. There is no overhanging turf and the grass between the trap and green is cut short. The ball is lying well upon the sand.

Choose your putter and stroke the ball off the sand and onto the green; or, play a short iron to the green. This should be a relatively trouble-free shot.

3. Your ball is lying either in a deep bunker with overhanging turf, or the ball is partially imbedded in soft sand. The sand trap is adjacent to the putting green. (fig. 8.1)

Use a wedge or the highest lofted iron you have. Open the club-face so it points skyward. For a firm stance work your feet well down into the sand. Play the ball in a position nearly opposite the left foot. If you desire, take an open stance. Depending upon the texture of the sand and the distance you want to hit the ball, aim to strike the sand one to three inches back of the ball. The clubhead should sweep into the sand and under the ball so there will be a cushion of sand between the club-face and the ball. Both the ball and some sand will be "splashed" out of the trap. Be certain to swing through the ball and sand in a smooth and continuous motion.

PLAYING HILLSIDE LIES

In playing from hillside lies, follow the adage—"don't make a mountain out of a molehill." Some players become completely wrapped up in only how to take their stance at the ball, and that is all they accomplish—the shot result is usually poor. They would be better off to trust their instinctive sense of feel to guide them in taking a comfortable stance in good balance. In stroking a ball from a slight, gentle slope, play the shot almost as you would any comparable shot from level ground. When playing from steeper hillside lies, you may find it necessary to make certain adjustments. Think *balance* for such shots: then (1) take a practice swing to register the feeling of maintaining good balance in the hillside stance; (2) settle down into a good stance and swing so you maintain your balance. Whatever your situation, try to keep your plans simple.

PLAYING SITUATIONS—Hole #8

Study each situation, 0-9, then plan the best way to play the shot. (You have the minimum set of 7 clubs recommended in the text)

1. Estimate the distance to the hole.
2. Determine and visualize the shot you desire.
3. Decide on the best club for the shot.
4. Are there particulars unique to the situation?

Imagine your ball in other positions and plan your strategy of play.

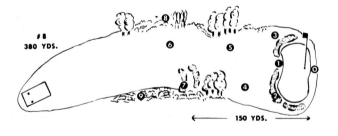

#8
380 YDS.

←——— 150 YDS. ———→

---

1. You have a *sidehill-uphill lie.* (fig. 8.2)

   Play the ball from a position favoring the higher side of the stance. To avoid accidentally causing the ball to move during the address, place the clubhead farther back of the ball than you normally do, or hold the club slightly above the ground. (If you cause the ball to move, it counts one stroke).

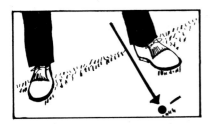

Fig. 8.2   Uphill lie

Fig. 8.3   Downhill lie

On long shots aim slightly to the right of the target, because in this situation there is a tendency to hit the ball to the left.

2. *You have a sidehill-downhill lie.* (fig. 8.3)

Play the ball from a position favoring the higher side of the stance. On long shots aim slightly to the left to counteract the tendency to push the ball to the right of the target. The ball will travel in a lower trajectory than normal so you may choose to use a higher lofted club.

3. *Your feet are on level ground; the ball is on level ground above your feet.*

You may find it best to grip down on the club handle. Take a practice swing to check on this. Aim slightly to the right to allow for the tendency to hit the ball to the left.

4. *Your feet are on level ground; the ball is on level ground below your feet.*

To help maintain balance during the swing, when you address the ball, settle your weight back toward your heels. Aim slightly left because of the tendency to hit the ball right.

Should your point of aim be to the left or to the right in each of the following situations: a sidehill-downhill lie; a crosswind from the left to right; you are standing on level ground with the ball lying on level ground below your feet?

PLAYING FROM THE ROUGH

Conditions in the rough vary. On some courses you can play the ball almost as you would play it from the fairway. Problems arise when you must hit the ball from long or heavy growth. In these situations your prime objective is to hit the ball out of the rough and onto a clear area. To get out of the rough be willing to sacrifice distance. Use a well-lofted club to get the ball into the air. If necessary, open the club-face. To avoid the interference of tall grass on the backswing, swing the clubhead in a more upright arc. Maintain a firm grip and complete the swing of the clubhead through the ball and grass. (In addressing the ball or in moving loose impediments, be careful that you do not accidentally move the ball and incur a penalty of one stroke).

PLAYING IN THE WIND

Playing golf in a strong wind is generally more difficult than playing on a calm day. Don't tense up trying to do the impossible. Adjust your scoring goals and your swing. Instead of taking a full swing for distance shots, try taking a shorter, more controlled swing. This may help you maintain your balance and stroke the ball more accurately.

When the wind is blowing the same direction as your intended long shots, take advantage of the situation—hit higher shots letting the wind carry the ball longer distances. Otherwise, try to hit low trajectory shots to avoid some of the wind interference. Don't fight the wind when you are hitting distance shots against it. If it is feasible, use a longer club for more distance, otherwise be satisfied with distance less than normal. If the wind is blowing across your line of play, aim your shot into the wind to allow for the carry of the ball in the wind direction.

To check the wind direction, note how the pennant on the flagstick is flying, or toss some blades of grass into the air and note the direction and force of the wind.

improving
your golf game
9

ATTITUDE AND CONCENTRATION

1. Your initial approach to golf must be that you, like thousands of others, can learn the game. Then after gaining some skill in stroking the ball you will develop the necessary confidence to play golf. This positive attitude cannot be fantasy. It must be something real, based on experience.

2. Golf requires concentration. But this does not mean taking a long time preparing to stroke the ball. Taking a lot of time may only be a subconscious stalling, an outcome of fear. Any plan of concentration should be simple. Plan your stroke, come to a definite decision, visualize the shot you desire, and proceed to execute the stroke.

3. Hitting good golf shots requires a certain amount of relaxation. Instead of attacking the game in a grim manner, try swinging the club gracefully and in good form. This is a key to stroking the ball well.

4. Good performance should be automatic. Faced with a certain shot, you will "feed" in necessary information, e.g., distance, mental picture of shot, etc., then like the computer you will "press the button" for automatic performance. You will tell yourself *what* to do—not *how* to do it.

5. If you hit one poor shot, do not hastily decide you are "off your game." A few poorly hit shots do not necessarily make a bad round. An error shot may be a blessing in disguise—you may make a brilliant recovery from a poor shot, which will stimulate you to play an excellent round.

6. Do not label yourself negatively as: "I can't putt," "I can't aim," "I can't use my 3-wood," etc. This could lead to poor play. Such statements made aloud are both boring and distracting to your fellow players.

7. Accept the responsibility for the shots you play. What someone else says or does should not affect your game adversely. Do not blame anyone or any bad break for a poor shot. Keep control of your game, then you can improve it.

8. The only strategy in competition is to play your own game. Players have been known to use schemes to upset their opponents, but this is not golf.

9. Golf requires perseverance and patience. When you are "off your game" do not allow yourself to be disheartened. Golf deflates our egos. It is forever challenging each of us to develop a sound, consistent game.

LESSONS

The pursuit of skill never ends. As long as you play golf you will take golf lessons—either from a golf teacher or from yourself in the form of self-coaching. This is the experience of all golfers, even the expert tournament professionals.

You will profit most from lessons if you follow certain practices.

1. Work with your instructor. When you are taking lessons do not work on pet theories of your own. To do an effective job of teaching, your instructor must know what you are trying to do.
2. When you are given a cue about your swing, do not expect a miracle to happen with the next shot. The result of a shot or two is not absolute proof of the worth or worthlessness of instruction.
3. After you receive a cue to change your swing, it may feel to you that you are following the cue and that your swing has changed drastically. For example, assume you have been swinging the club back beyond the horizontal position. The instructor asks you to take a three-quarter swing, and you take what "feels" to be that length swing. Your instructor tells you the shaft was again swung beyond the horizontal. The changes you feel do not necessarily match what actually happens.
4. In a golf class general instruction in the fundamentals and some individual coaching will be given. There is good reason for individual help—all swings do not develop the same. The coaching given another person may not be useful to you.
5. Do not be disappointed and feel that you are not getting your "money's worth" if your instructor implies or says your swing looks fine and what you need is practice and play, not more instruction in swing analysis.

SELF-COACHING

Intelligent self-coaching builds your golf game; poor self-coaching destroys it. Your future golf game might be influenced most by your self-teaching.

1. If you find yourself with a persistent problem, you will probably save yourself much frustration and time if you take a lesson from a competent teacher instead of continuing to work alone.
2. You can gather a mass of data on the golf swings—from reading, taking lessons, watching expert golfers in action, and listening to other players. Be intelligent and discriminating in evaluating these ideas. Are the concepts sound and do they apply to you? Accumulating information has a bad and good side: you may "jam" your brain with too much data, or you may be enlightened by a new and different approach to the swing.
3. If you are having trouble with a particular shot or club, do not decide that you will proceed with correcting and mastering this problem only.

If other shots are being hit well, the error may be mental. You actually prevent yourself from performing well by expecting a poor result. Put the club away and forget it. Work on strokes you are hitting well, then go back to your "problem" for short practice periods.

4. You cannot avoid the experience common to all golfers—going into a slump. This may be the result of either some error in your stroke or it may be mental. Do not panic and look for gross errors in your swing. Concentrate on what to do *right*, not on "What am I doing wrong?" Go back to the *basics*: check your grip, stance, and address position; work on a smooth, rhythmic stroke; work on good form. Practice the short approach shots and work up to longer shots.

5. The hands are the connecting link with the club. They must direct, control, and transmit power. A player who has a fine sense of control with his fingers and hands will stroke the ball well. The hands should work together as a unit and coordinate all movements that make up the swing. Sense the hands directing and controlling the clubhead action.

6. Theories for hitting golf shots and correcting swings abound. You can go to a practice range and get "free" lessons by asking almost any player for advice. The value of these lessons can be questioned. Many golfers like to tell their "secrets of success." Their advice varies from day to day. A tip that seems a miraculous cure one day is discarded the next.

A HOME PRACTICE PLAN

Through practice swinging and exercises you can train yourself to move in good form. You can deposit correct movements in your "muscle memory bank."

Here is a starting program. Make adaptations as you see fit, but keep the plan simple—complicated exercise programs are quickly abandoned and forgotten. Gradually increase the times you swing and do the exercises. Use your good judgment on what is a worthwhile work-out for you. (see also Ch. 4-7 Practice Suggestions)

1. Practice the putting stroke without and with a ball.
2. Swing a club without hitting balls. Practice taking the one-quarter, one-half, three-quarter, and full swings.
3. Make the club a familiar tool by handling it. (fig. 9.1)
   a. Draw air circles, figure 8's, etc., with the clubhead.
   b. Lightly tap the ground with the clubhead. Direct your attention to moving the clubhead, not the handle—like lightly pounding a nail with a hammer—use the "striker." Do the same exercise holding the club with only one hand and then the other. Lengthen the tapping stroke.
   c. Point the clubhead forward and then back over your right shoulder. Keep the left arm easily extended and let the right elbow bend. Note the responsive wrist action.
4. Make a moving machine of your legs and body. (fig. 9.2)
   a. Practice the foot and leg exercise.
   b. Without using a club take the posture of addressing the ball. Swing your arms back and forth continuously letting your legs and body re-

Fig. 9.1 Exercises—handling club   Fig. 9.2 Exercises—body motion

---

From a target, pace off or measure distances of 20, 30, and 40 yards. Practice both chip shots and pitch shots from these distances.

1. Note the lengths of the swings you must take for the different shots.
2. Test your accuracy in hitting the shots. Hit a total of 30 balls, 10 from each distance. How many balls come to rest within 7 paces (approximately 20 feet) of the hole or target?
3. Check your progress. Keep a mental or written record of your practice.

---

spond to the arm swing. Increase the motion so one shoulder swings under your chin and then the other. Maintain the posture of addressing the ball.

c. Hold the club-shaft horizontally at mid-thigh height and take the posture of addressing the ball. Swing your arms back and forth, pointing one end of the shaft toward the ground and then the other. Let your weight shift from one foot to the other. Keep a good balance.

d. Practice the pivot while holding the club-shaft horizontally at shoulder height. Check your form by doing the exercises in front of a mirror.

EXAMINATION OF SOME ERROR SHOTS

Topping

A topped ball is hit above its center, thus imparting topspin to the ball. (fig. 9.3) The ball may travel in the air a short distance and then dive to the ground, or it may just roll along the ground.

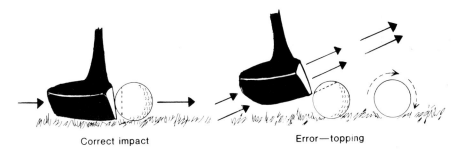

Correct impact   Error—topping

Fig. 9.3

The commonly heard correction for topping is "keep your head down." At times this cue may work, but it is so limited in scope that the adoption of this idea only can be questionable. Can you keep your head (cranium) down and still top the ball? Of course you can, because only the clubhead tops the ball. Raising the head is more the result of, not the cause of, topping. When a ball is topped the clubhead action through the impact zone is upward. This action tends to force your head and body to move up. The body weight may not shift to the left foot, and in extreme cases, there may be a shift of weight to the right foot with the left heel raising from the ground. This strange form is the result of the erroneous effort of swinging upward. Another reason a player raises his head is that he changes his focus of attention from the execution of the shot to its result. Because of tension and anxiety he looks up quickly to see what happened to the ball. These are reasons why "keep your head down" is not the complete answer to the problems of striking a golf ball.

To correct topping, center your attention on the cause of the error (club-face and ball contact) not on the result of the error.

1. Ask yourself: "What am I trying to do?" If you are trying to "hit the ball into the air" or "get under the ball," then you have selected the wrong purpose. Hit the ball squarely and let the club-face loft the ball.

2. If you will try to hit the ball so that it will travel in a low trajectory, the clubhead should travel low through the contact area; thus the chances are good that correct club face and ball contact will be made.
3. In the address position, instead of looking at the top of the ball, watch a spot at the back of the ball where contact should be made.
4. Do not tense your shoulders and arms in the impact zone, thereby drawing the club in toward you and away from the ball.
5. If the ball is hit from a tee, sweep out the tee as you strike the ball. If the ball is hit from the grass, sweep the grass after the ball is struck. Practice swinging without a ball, keeping the clubhead low and sweeping the grass through the impact zone.

Striking the Ground Before Ball Contact—"Fat" Shot

This error may be related to topping if an attempt is made to "scoop" the ball into the air. Quick, violent exertions in the impact area can also result in "fat" shots. To correct the error, discard any purpose of trying to "scoop" the ball into the air. Once a player hits several "fat" shots, especially short pitch shots, a feeling of apprehension arises when another such shot must be played. Such fears can be dispelled and the error corrected by practice on the practice range. (See chapter 5: Grip, Hand Action, and Wrist Action; also fig. 9.4.)

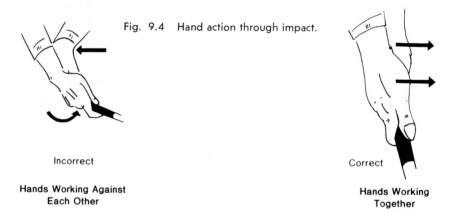

Fig. 9.4   Hand action through impact.

Incorrect

**Hands Working Against
Each Other**

Correct

**Hands Working
Together**

Shanking the Ball

If shanking the ball were a common fault, the population of golfers might decrease considerably. Shanking may be the most ornery error in golf. This shot is hit with an iron and the ball is contacted near the neck of the club, the rounded surface at the heel of the club face. When the ball is struck with this rounded surface, the ball "squirts" out to the right. The feeling the player experiences is horrendous, one of total ineffectiveness. There are fortunate golfers who have never or rarely shanked a shot. Those unfortunate players who go through periods of shanking might do better seeing a psychiatrist than seeing a golf teacher. The word "shank" is taboo in golf conversa-

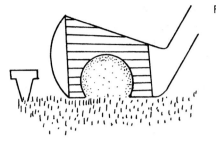

Fig. 9.5   Avoiding a shank.

tion—golfers fear that mention of the word will bring on the error! Opinions on corrections vary and volumes could be written on the subject. The following are possible corrections.

1. Go back to the simple—practice hitting short approach shots with a medium iron and work up to longer iron shots. Unless your swing is completely off, this may be your best correction—working on the positive and not fighting a fault.

2. When shanking occurs the clubhead is outside of the correct path at ball contact. Picking up the club on the backswing, extra effort at the start of the downswing, and extra effort through impact could all force the clubhead outside of the correct arc. To help keep the clubhead on the correct path at impact, place a tee in the ground beyond the ball outside the clubhead path. When you strike the ball, avoid hitting the tee, thereby keeping the clubhead on the correct path and making correct ball contact (fig. 9.5).

3. Check the spot on the club-face where you are addressing the ball. Addressing the ball out toward the toe of the club-face to allow for any error may be of temporary help.

EXAMINATION OF DIRECTIONAL FLIGHT ERRORS

Why a golf shot travels off line to the right or left of the intended target should not be a mystery. To demonstrate how you can stroke a ball off line try this experiment using a putter. Putt a ball to a target about five feet away. Then keeping the same stance and grip, putt a ball to the right of the target. Now stroke a ball so it will roll to the left of the original target. If the ball rolled straight to the right or left, the putter face was at right angles to the clubhead path. If the ball rolled with clockwise or counter-clockwise spin, then the club-face was not perpendicular to the path of the club.

If you play baseball or softball, you can hit balls to left, center, and right fields. Depending upon the field into which you want the ball to travel, you time your swing so that the bat faces the target at impact. No change of stance is necessary. If you play tennis or table tennis, you hit shots to right, center, or left courts. If you see your opponent out of position, at one side of the court, you direct your shot to the opposite side of the court. You may even purposely put some side spin on the ball to deceive your opponent. You

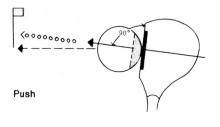

Push

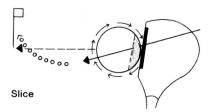

Slice

Push—Straight shot to right of target
- Clubhead path through impact is on a line toward the right of the target—from inside-out.
- Club face is perpendicular to the clubhead path.

Slice—Ball curves to right due to clockwise (horizontal) spin
- Clubhead path through impact can be: (1) On a line to the target, (2) From outside-in, (3) From inside-out.
- Club face is pointing to the right of the clubhead path.

Fig. 9.6   Push and slice

know through experience that the position of the hitting surface and the path of the striking implement through the contact area determines the flight of the ball. This is basic information to use when examining errors in directional flight of the golf ball (see Ch. 3, fig. 3.3).

Push and Slice

Both shots travel to the right of the intended target. In a *push shot* the path of the clubhead through the contact area is on a line toward the right of the target and the club-face is perpendicular to this line. This produces a straight shot but off line to the right. In a *slice*, the path of the clubhead through contact can vary, but the club-face in relation to the path is open or facing to the right. This contact produces a horizontal, clockwise spin on the ball. As the spinning ball travels through the air, the ball will curve to the right (fig. 9.6). In considering corrections for these errors assume that the grip and stance are correct and the golf swing in general appears to be one of good form. There are no unusual or outstanding obvious distortions in swinging the club. If this is true, the error is produced by incorrect efforts in the contact area.

1. One of the main reasons for hitting to the right is trying to put something extra into the shot. Instead of swinging the club-face to the square position the handle is pushed, thus changing either the path of the club, the club-face, or both. Develop the feeling of swinging the clubhead *through* the contact area.

2. When you become anxious and fearful of the shot result, you tend to stop the swing of the clubhead through impact, thereby leaving the club-face open, and looking up quickly to see the shot result. This is called "coming off the ball" and can result in hitting to the right.

3. Do not try to get a straight follow-through with the clubhead or to "steer" the ball to the target. The result of such action is usually a hit off line to

the right. Trust that the clubhead will travel in the correct path and strike the ball squarely.

4. Do not allow for any error to the right by aiming to the left of your target. You will only compound the error.

5. If you have been swinging with the club face open at contact, it may "feel" that the club face is closed when you swing it to the square position. Because of this "feel" already established, you may actually have to attempt to swing the face to a closed position to reach the square position. Do not be fearful of trying to do this. If after trying the correction the ball travels straight, then you know that the face was square even if it "felt" closed to you. If the ball travels to the left then an overcorrection was made, thus producing a hook or pull.

An often-heard correction for slicing is "hit from inside out." This may have some value for the person who has a very distorted swing with the clubhead travelling from way outside and across the intended line of flight. This is not the error of most people. Following only the cue, "swing from inside out," may increase the error of hitting to the right. The path of the clubhead through the contact area should be from inside the intended line—on the intended line—and then inside again.

A closed stance is suggested frequently to correct slicing. If the player takes a closed stance and has a feeling he is aiming to the right, and then compensates for this aim by swinging the club-face over to direct the ball to the intended target, this stance would be an aid. But changing the stance does not necessarily change the direction of the shot—trick shot artists prove this. They can take any stance, stand on one foot, or even sit down and hit the ball any direction they choose. The path of the clubhead through the impact area and the relation of the club-face to this path determines the directional flight of the ball.

Pull and Hook

Both shots travel to the left of the intended target. In the *pull shot* the path of the clubhead through the contact area is on a line toward the left of the target and the club-face is perpendicular to this line. This produces a straight shot but off line to the left. In a *hook shot* the path of the clubhead can vary, but the club-face in relation to the clubhead path is closed or facing to the left. This contact produces a horizontal counter-clockwise spin of the ball. As the spinning ball travels through the air, the ball will curve to the left (fig. 9.7). The errors of pulling and hooking are less common than those of pushing and slicing. Consider the following in correcting the pull or hook.

1. An incorrect grip with either one or both hands shifted more to the right than normal, right palm facing more skyward, left palm facing more toward the ground, can cause error shots to the left. (A grip in reverse of this, with either or both hands positioned more to the left, can cause error shots to the right.) (fig. 9.8)

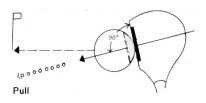

Pull

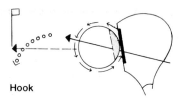

Hook

Pull—Straight shot to left of target
• Clubhead path through impact is on a line toward the left of the target—from outside-in.
• Club face is perpendicular to clubhead path.

Hook—Ball curves to left due to counterclockwise (horizontal) spin
• Clubhead path through impact can be: (1) On a line to the target, (2) From inside-out, (3) From outside-in.
• Club face is pointing to the left of the clubhead path.

Fig. 9.7 Pull and hook

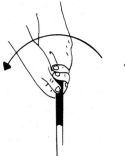

Fig. 9.8

Grip favoring shot
to left—draw

Grip favoring shot
to right—fade

2. Trying to hit the ball an extra long distance and "slapping" at the ball often results in hooking the ball. The right hand overpowers the left in the impact zone, thus closing the club-face. When this error is corrected the player may sense a dramatic change in the swing. He may feel that the left hand and arm are in control of the downswing and follow-through, and that the right hand is doing little or nothing to strike the ball. He may feel that he is not "hitting the ball as hard" as he can.

3. If there is a consistent error of pulling the ball to the left of the target, check the stance and the ball position in relation to the feet. When a player pulls a ball it may be obvious that he has turned his body too early in the impact zone. Fear of hitting to the right may cause a player to turn on the ball to direct the ball away from an error shot to the right.

Skilled players will at times intentionally strike a ball so that it curves in flight and ends up on target. The draw shot curves in flight from right to left; the fade shot curves in flight from left to right.

You strike the ball so that the club-face compresses the side of the ball beyond its center and the club-face is closed in relation to its path through the ball. How will the ball react? What are these shots called?

PLAYING HINTS

1. Be ready to play golf. Warm up before you play: start your practice with the short swings, gradually working to the full swings. Do gentle stretching exercises for relaxation. The greatest area of tension for most people is through the neck and shoulders. Make easy movements and do stretches that will relax these areas. As you play your round of golf stay "easy" so you can use your muscles efficiently when swinging the club.

2. Learn the golf rules. Ignorance of the rules may cost you penalty strokes. Privileges extended by the rules may prove advantageous, i.e., when you drop a ball back of a water hazard, you may choose a well-kept area of grass on which to drop the ball, provided all the other provisions of the rules are followed.

3. Play according to the rules and keep your score accurately. To do otherwise is deceiving yourself.

4. Golf should be a congenial and friendly game. When all players are considerate of each other, the game is enjoyable. The golf course is not the place for a lot of talk and idle chatter. You might ask yourself: "Whose game am I most interested in?" You know that answer, and it is the same for all other golfers.

5. In your early games of golf, improving the lie of the ball on the fairway may be condoned. However, after you have developed your game, play the ball as it lies, according to the rules. Continued play of winter rules is not golf and will make stroking the ball difficult when you are required to play by the official rules.

6. Do not complain about the course you are playing. You choose the course, it does not choose you.

7. During a round of golf no instruction should be given. If you are having a bad day, accept it. Do not seek advice from another player. Also, do not offer to teach someone or to give playing tips.

8. Assume you are teeing off. There is an out of bounds along the right side of the fairway. Tee your ball toward the right side of the teeing area and aim to the center or slightly left of center of the fairway. Whenever you can, use this strategy of aiming away from trouble when teeing off.

9. The interference of a wooden tee can prevent an effective golf shot. For example, if you tee off with a lofted iron the tee and the ball might be contacted simultaneously (fig. 9.9). This contact can deflect or slow

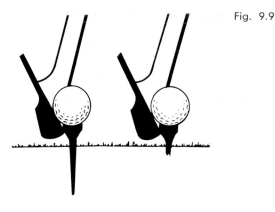

Fig. 9.9

down the clubhead. When you tee off with an iron, use a broken tee that barely goes into the ground. Should the clubhead strike the tee, it will fly out of the ground with the hit and offer no resistance. Whenever you do use a long wooden tee in hard ground, loosen the turf around the tee, as you place the tee into the ground

10. To avoid tension, do not overrespond to a situation. For example, you see your ball roll into a distant sand trap. Do not react immediately in concern over playing the next shot. When you reach the sand trap, size up the situation, plan the shot, and play it.

11. When you play golf, choose the correct club for a shot by considering:
    a. The *lie* of the ball on the ground.
    b. The *distance* you want to strike the ball.
    c. The *situation*, such as whether you have to hit the ball in a high or a low trajectory, etc.
    d. The course *conditions*, such as wind directions; wet, soft, or dried out turf; etc.
    e. Your *skill* with the different clubs. If there is a choice between clubs, choose the club in which you have the most confidence.

12. Learn different distances to the green by spotting various objects, such as trees, bushes, sand traps. Learn the breaks of the greens. Figure out and remember the most advantageous ways to play each hole. Adjust your game to the course you are playing. For example, do not try to hit pitch shots to hard greens. When the greens will not hold pitch shots and it is not necessary to loft the ball into the air, hit low run-up shots.

13. If the ball is lying in a difficult position—on sparse grass or on bare ground, take a practice swing over a spot similar in nature (if such a spot is near your ball). You have then faced the situation and are less apt to be concerned about hitting from a poor lie.

14. Do not hesitate to play a safe shot when a daring one may get you into trouble. If playing a safe shot costs you an extra stroke, you may possibly make it up with a one-putt green.

15. Play your own game of golf. If your distance limit for a 7-iron is 120 yards, do not be challenged to hit a 7-iron 140 yards because a member

of your foursome can do so. Your objective is to score well, not to hit a shot a certain distance.

16. Keep a record of your putts. In a corner of the scoring square for each hole, place a number indicating putts for the hole.

17. Study your game after a round. Where did you use poor judgment in playing a shot? How many putts did you take? How many times was your approach shot to the green short of the hole? How many times was your first putt short of the hole? What part of your game needs improvement? What shots need the most practice?

essential knowledge
10

If you are a novice you cannot expect to hit the ball like the experienced player, but you can put yourself in this class in some respects. You can gain knowledge of the game and practice correct procedures of conduct. You can become "well-informed." Supplement the following information by studying the official rule book and other golf books, and by carefully observing experienced players on the course. Be willing and ready to learn, and you will be a welcome member of any golfing group.

ETIQUETTE

The rules of etiquette are not strict formalities that complicate play. They simplify and enhance the game. Observance of these rules makes it possible to play better golf and enjoy the game more, to keep the course in good playing condition, and to allow more people to play golf by speeding up play.

Playing good golf requires concentration. Etiquette and good sportsmanship thus require that you respect and do not distract the player making a stroke. Always stand quietly and out of range of the player when he is addressing the ball or taking a stroke. Do not stand directly behind the ball or directly behind the hole.

Care of the Golf Course

1. Replace any divot and press it firmly in place. Avoid taking divots with practice swings.
2. Walk carefully on the putting green to avoid marring the surface. Do not step or stand at the edge of the hole (cup).
3. Do not drop or throw the flagstick on the green.
4. If you use a golf cart, keep it well away from the apron of the putting green.
5. Repair ball marks on the putting green. A golf tee can be used, but a better device is a fork-like metal tool—these are available at a nominal

cost. Lift up and press back the grass around the pit mark leaving a level surface.
6. If you drive a motorized cart on the course, stay on the paved cart paths as much as possible. Never drive between a green and any adjacent sand trap. Keep carts well away from the greens.
7. When leaving a bunker, smooth out the surface so that its condition is as good as or better than when you entered it.
8. Do not discard any litter on the course. Do your part in maintaining the beauty of the golf course.

Playing Without Delay

1. When you pay your green fee, remember you are one of many paying for the privilege of playing on the course.
2. Be ready to play. Have a knowledge of safety, etiquette, and rules and possess basic skills in the strokes.
3. You will need your own set of clubs, golf bag, balls, and tees. Do not borrow clubs from another player. Carry your own golf bag. Do not be burdened with extra items such as purses and sweaters. Place them in the golf bag or check them at the pro shop.
4. Identify your ball before starting play. Check to see that you are not playing the same make and ball number as another player in your group. When your ball is in play, as on the fairway, do not pick up the ball for identification. Simply look around it and check the make and number. If it appears that a player in the distance is going to play your ball by mistake, call "fore" and wave to him.
5. Avoid delaying play by taking numerous practice swings.
6. Be ready to take your stroke when it is your turn. It is possible to plan ahead for some strokes. (See chap. 7—Putting)
7. Any instruction should be incidental. There should not be any delay because one person is attempting to teach another.
8. When you hit a ball, spot its position carefully. Spot its position in relation to some stationary object so you can walk directly to it. Watch the stroke results of other players in your group so you can help in any search for a ball.
9. If you, as a novice, find yourself in some difficult situation, e.g., unable to hit from a deep bunker after making several attempts, pick up the ball and drop it out of the bunker. Your scores for your early games of golf are not so important that they merit your delaying the play of others.
10. When your ball is on the wrong fairway, permit players playing that hole to have the right of way. Some courses have a local rule allowing you to lift the ball from the wrong fairway and drop it in the correct fairway. Safety and speeding up play make this an acceptable local rule.
11. If your group is delaying play by failing to keep its place, losing more than one clear hole on the players in front, invite the following group to pass. In turn, if you are extended this courtesy, express your appreciation.

12. When someone in your group is searching for his ball, help in the search. Invite following players to play through.

13. At some golf courses on par 3 holes, signs are posted directing golfers who have reached the putting green to invite players of the following group to hit their tee shots. When you follow this procedure, be certain you do not stand in line with the flagstick. Stand behind the green and off the putting surface. Standing in this position you will not disturb the players shooting onto the green, and you will be relatively safe. However, do watch the shots of the players in case someone overshoots the green. After the players have hit their tee shots, your foursome proceeds to putt out.

14. In match play and in recreational play golfers often concede putts of 8 to 10 inches or less to their playing companions. For example, Player A plays his third stroke and his ball comes to rest 5 inches from the hole. A playing companion may say, "That's good," pick up the ball, and toss it back to Player A. Player A scores a 4 on the hole. The time required for putting out is thus saved.

15. In "recreational" golf strict adherence to the rule requiring the ball farthest from the hole to be played first is being relaxed. In the interests of faster play there is justification for this relaxation of the rule. Examples: (a) Three people of a foursome are on the putting green. The fourth player, A, is shooting from a sand trap adjacent to the green. He hits a poor shot to the far side of the green, and his ball is farthest from the hole. It will take time for Player A to rake the trap and then walk to his ball. Instead of waiting for A to play first, one or more of the other players is probably ready to putt and should proceed to do so. (b) You are ready to play your ball from the left side of the fairway, 150 yards from the hole. Your playing companion, B, is searching for his ball in the right rough, 160 yards from the hole. Since you are ready, it is acceptable for you to go ahead and play your shot, even though you are not away. After you play your stroke you may wish to walk over and help Player B in search for his ball. Many players follow these and similar procedures to speed up play.

On the Putting Green

1. Place golf bag or cart well off of and on the side of the green nearest the next tee.

2. Whether a ball be on or off the putting green, the rules state that the ball farthest from the hole be played. The trend in "recreational" play is to allow golfers off the putting surface—whether or not they are farthest from the hole—to play first. This practice can save time because the possible necessity of alternately attending the flagstick or leaving the flagstick unattended is eliminated.

3. Do not step or stand in any line of play. Do not allow your shadow to be cast in someone's line of play.

4. Mark and lift your ball when requested to do so. To mark your ball's position, place a small coin or marker behind the ball and then lift the ball. If your ball is in a direct line of play, measure the necessary lengths of the putter head to one side of the line and place the marker at this spot. In stroke play the USGA recommends that the ball nearer the hole be played, rather than marked and lifted, provided subsequent play of a fellow competitor is not affected. In stroke play a player has the option of either marking or playing his ball. If in playing the ball you would have to stand in another player's line of putt, mark and lift your ball, do NOT take your stance in another player's line of putt. This option of "continuous putting" (instead of marking balls lying near the cup) helps speed up play.
5. When holding the flagstick, stand to one side of the hole and hold both the stick and the pennant. The stick should be held in the hole until removal is necessary. Stand so that your shadow does not cast across the line of play. After removal of the flagstick, lay it down out of play. When all players are on the putting green or close to it, a player whose ball lies close to the hole generally offers to attend the flagstick.
6. For your safety and to avoid delaying play, after your group has holed out, replace the flagstick, leave the green immediately, and proceed to the next tee. Do not stand on the green either to review play of the hole or to mark your scores on the score card.

In the Bunker (Sand Trap)

1. Leave the bag or cart well outside the edge of the bunker.
2. Enter the sand trap at the lowest bank and take the shortest route to the ball.
3. Before you walk into a bunker, check to see if the rake is nearby. If it is not, secure it and place it near you, where it will not interfere with play. With the rake close at hand, you can rake the sand as you are walking out of the trap.
4. Do not enter or stand in a bunker when another golfer is playing from it.
5. On leaving the sand trap, rake or in some manner smooth out all footprints and marks you have made.

RULES

This is a summary of certain rules. This knowledge together with the rules of etiquette will enable you to play golf properly. This digest of rules, however, is no substitute for the official rules.*

*The official rules may be obtained from your local golf club or from the United States Golf Association, Far Hills, New Jersey 07931

Types of Competition

Some rules differ for the two types of competition, *stroke play and match play*. Most golf played is stroke play. In this competition the winner is the person with the lowest score for the stipulated number of rounds, usually four rounds, a total of 72 holes. If two or more players are tied for first place at the end of the tournament, the USGA recommends that these players play an 18-hole round to determine the winner. In most tournaments, however, players tied for first place play one or more extra holes, and the first player to make the low score on a hole is the winner. The terms *competitor* and *fellow-competitor* are used to describe the contestants in stroke play.

Match play competition is based on scores for each hole, not total score for a round. In a match a person competes against only one other player, his *opponent*. They play until one person is more holes ahead than there are holes remaining to be played in the match. If the match is tied at the end of a round, the players continue play until one player wins a hole. Match play is an elimination type tournament, so in the final round there are only two players remaining to compete for the championship.

Match Play Score Card

Assume that at the end of nine holes Bill is 1 hole up on Joe. Hole #10 is tied or *halved*. Bill remains 1 up. Joe wins #11. The match is *all square*. Joe wins #12 and #13. Joe is 2 up. Hole #14 is halved. Joe wins #15. Joe is *dormie 3*. A player is dormie when he is the same number of holes up as there are holes remaning to be played. Hole #16 is halved. Joe wins the match, 3 holes up with 2 remaining, or simply 3 and 2 (3-2).

HOLE NO.	10	11	12	13	14	15	16	17	18
Bill (1 up)	5	5	4	7	4	4	4	—	
	o	-	-	-	o	-	o		
Joe (1 down)	5	3	3	5	4	3	4	—	
	o	+	+	+	o	+	o		

Fig. 10.1 Match play card

Rules for Teeing Off

1. Play is started on each hole by teeing the ball within the limits of the teeing area. This area is bounded in front by two tee markers and extends two club lengths back of the markers.
2. If in addressing the ball you accidentally knock it off the tee, you may replace it without penalty.
3. Honor, the privilege of teeing first, is decided by lot on the first tee. After the first hole, the honor is decided by scores on the previous hole. The person with the lowest score plays first and the others follow according to scores. If two or more players score the same on a hole, they tee off in the order they followed on the last tee.

General Rules

1. After teeing off you continue striking the ball until you hole out. The ball should be played as it lies and not be touched except to strike it, unless situations or rules require or allow you to do otherwise.
2. You play in turn so the ball farthest from the hole is played first. (Exception: Stroke play, "continuous putting" on green—see Etiquette—Putting Green. Also, other exceptions may be made in stroke play to speed up play.)
3. Any attempt to hit the ball is counted as a stroke, whether or not the ball is struck.
4. If you accidentally move the ball in play or cause it to move, this counts as a stroke. (Exception, Rule 35 1b — If you move loose impediments on the putting green and the ball is moved, you may replace the ball without penalty.)
5. If such loose impediments as fallen leaves and pebbles interfere with your play of the ball, you may move them, but they may not be moved from a hazard.
6. When the ball is in play, you cannot press or stamp down the ground near the ball or break or bend anything growing.
7. Movable obstructions (water hoses, trash containers, etc.) that interfere with play may be removed. If the ball is moved in so doing, it shall be replaced without penalty.
8. If your ball lies in, on, or so close to an immovable obstruction (paved cart path, sprinkler head, ball washer, etc.) that interferes with your stance or area of intended swing, you may, without penalty, lift and drop the ball within one club length of the nearest point of relief, not nearer the hole.
9. To drop a ball, face the hole, stand erect, and drop the ball behind you over your shoulder. The ball must not come to rest nearer the hole.
10. If your ball lies on the wrong putting green, you must lift the ball and drop it off the green. Drop it within one club length of the nearest point of relief, not nearer the hole. (No penalty).
11. If your ball lies in or touches casual water, ground under repair, or a hole made by a burrowing animal—or, if such conditions interfere with your stance or area of intended swing, you may obtain relief as follows:
    a. Through the green, you may lift and drop the ball within one club length of the nearest point of relief, not nearer the hole, without penalty.
    b. In a hazard, you may without penalty, lift and drop the ball in the hazard as near as possible to where the ball lay, not nearer the hole; or, under penalty of one stroke, drop the ball outside the hazard, not nearer the hole, keeping the spot where the ball lay between yourself and the hole.

    c. On the putting green, if such conditions interfere or intervene between your ball lying on the green and the hole, you may lift and place (not drop) the ball at the nearest point of relief, not nearer the hole, without penalty.

12. You may ask only your caddie, partner, or partner's caddie for advice regarding the playing of a stroke.
13. If another player's ball interferes with your play, you may request that he mark and lift the ball.
14. There is some difference in the penalties for the breach of a rule. (Refer to the official rule book.) The general penalty for breaking a rule is two strokes in stroke play and loss of a hole in match play. (See #5 and #6 above) If you remove loose impediments from a hazard or stamp down the grass back of the ball in play, it will cost you two strokes in stroke play, and you will immediately lose the hole in match play.
15. The score card should be checked for local rules and interpretations which apply to the course being played.

Rules for the Putting Green

1. When playing your ball on the putting green, request that the flagstick be attended or removed from the hole. The penalty for your ball, played from the putting green, striking the flagstick is two strokes in stroke play and loss of hole in match play.
2. In stroke play, when you play your ball on the putting green and your ball strikes a fellow competitor's ball, also on the putting green, the penalty is two strokes. If this impact moves the fellow competitor's ball, he must replace it.
3. In match play, if your ball strikes your opponent's ball there is no penalty. Your opponent has the option of replacing his ball or leaving it where it comes to rest.
4. There is a rule governing the putting stance. Imagine the line of putt extending from the hole to a point beyond the ball position. You cannot take a stance with either foot straddling or touching that extended imaginary line. (Rules 35 IL)

Rules for Hazards

1. By USGA definition there are two types of hazards: bunkers and water hazards. A bunker usually is a depressed area of bare ground covered with sand, frequently called a sand trap. Grass-covered area surrounding the bunker is not part of the hazard. The grass-covered area or any dry ground surrounding a water hazard may be part of the hazard. Local rules will determine the limits of water hazards.
2. Loose impediments may not be moved from a hazard.
3. Man-made objects, such as a rake, may be moved.
4. In addressing the ball in a hazard, you may not ground the club. You may not touch the surface of the hazard with the clubhead before taking your forward swing to strike the ball.
5. If you lose a ball in a water hazard or find it impossible to play the ball from the hazard you may: (A) drop a ball, under penalty of one stroke,

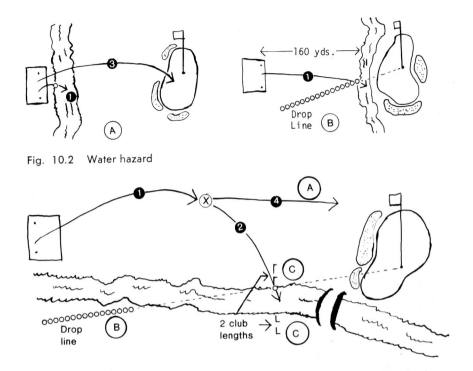

Fig. 10.2   Water hazard

Fig. 10.3   Lateral water hazard

at the spot from which the original ball was played; if the original ball was played from the tee, the ball may be teed anywhere in the teeing area; or, (B) drop a ball, under penalty of one stroke, any distance behind the hazard, keeping the spot at which the ball last crossed the margin of the hazard between you and the hole. In situation A, figure 10.2, it is to your advantage to tee the ball again. In situation B, figure 10.2, you would lose too much yardage if you played again from the tee. Therefore you would usually drop a ball any distance back of the hazard, keeping the spot at which the ball last crossed the margin of the hazard between you and the hole. (Note line on which to drop ball.)

6. For a lateral water hazard you may play your next stroke in accordance with (A) or (B) in #5 above; or, (C) under penalty of one stroke, you may drop a ball within two club lengths of either side of the hazard, opposite the point where the ball last crossed the margin of the hazard, but not nearer the hole. (See fig. 10.3. Option A, drop ball at X. Option B, drop ball on line indicated. Option C, drop ball within 2 club lengths of either side of the hazard.)

Ball Out of Bounds, Lost, or Unplayable

1. A ball is out of bounds when it lies on ground on which play is prohibited. The area is usually marked by a fence or out of bound stakes.
2. You are allowed five minutes to search for a ball. After that time the ball is deemed lost.

3. If your ball is out of bounds or is lost outside a water hazard, the penalty is loss of distance and one stroke. You play your next stroke at the spot from which the original ball was played and add one penalty stroke. (fig. 10.4)

4. If you declare your ball unplayable, you may (a) proceed under the stroke and distance rule (#3 above); or under penalty of one stroke you may either (b) drop your ball within two club lengths of the unplayable position, but not nearer the hole; or (c) drop the ball any distance behind the unplayable position, keeping that point between yourself and the hole. You are the sole judge as to when your ball is unplayable.

5. When you hit a ball that you think might be out of bounds or might be lost outside a water hazard, to save time you may at once play a *provisional ball*. If the original ball is playable, you play it and pick up the provisional ball. If the original ball is out of bounds or lost, then you continue play with the provisional ball. The penalty (see #3) applies.

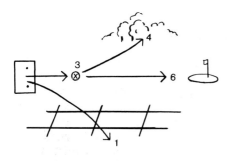

Fig. 10.4 Stroke and distance rule

Stroke and Distance Rule (See fig. 10.4)

A player drives out of bounds (1). He tees another ball, adds a penalty stroke and shoots 3 from the tee. From the fairway he shoots his fourth shot into the rough and loses the ball. He drops a ball at spot (X), adds a penalty stroke and shoots stroke 6.

What is the purpose of handicapping and how is a handicap established? What does the term "scratch golfer" mean?

HANDICAPS

A handicap is a number representing approximately the strokes a player shoots over par for a round. For instance, if a player has a handicap of 2, he is an excellent golfer; if he has a handicap of 30, he is a novice. A player who has a handicap of 0 averages near par and is called a scratch golfer.

To establish a handicap* a given number of rounds are played, usually 20. Score cards are turned in to the golf club or association and the handicap is figured from the 10 lowest scores of the 20.

Handicaps are used to equalize competitive play. In an 18-hole stroke play handicap event, a net score is computed for each player by subtracting his handicap from the actual (gross) score. The player with the low net score is the winner.

In match play the player with the higher handicap is allowed to subtract from his score on certain holes. For example, two opponents have handicaps of 7 and 4. The player with the 7 handicap subtracts one stroke from each of his scores on the three holes with a handicap rating of 1, 2, and 3. On the score card (Ch. 1, fig. 1.2), the three holes rated most difficult are #6, #14, and #9 for men, and #3, #17, and #5 for women. The player with the handicap of 4 gives the 7 handicapper one stroke on each of these holes, if the full handicap difference is allowed.

Honest and up-to-date handicaps make competition between players of unequal ability possible and enjoyable.

SELECTION OF EQUIPMENT AND ACCESSORIES

The amount of money you wish to invest in golf will determine your selection of equipment and accessories. Your initial investment can be a small one or a considerable one. Used sets of clubs and used golf balls are available, and minimum sets of new clubs and new balls are marketed at reasonable prices. A variety of new, high quality matched sets of clubs offer a wide selection to the person wishing to make a substantial investment in clubs. Generally the more expensive clubs will have more "feel." Higher quality material is used in their construction, and the time is taken to match the shafts and clubheads to insure better balance.

Because of the differences in height, strength, and hand size between men and women, men's clubs are longer, have stronger and stiffer shafts, have larger grips, and are heavier. The average golfer will find the medium shaft best suits his needs. The person with above average power and strength might find a shaft stiffer than medium better, while a person with average or less strength and power may be helped by a more flexible shaft.

Two weight measurements are considered in fitting clubs—total weight and swing weight. Simply stated swing weight is a measurement of the clubhead weight in proportion to the shaft and grip weight. The swing weight of women's clubs ranges from C-0 to C-9. C-0 to C-2 are light clubs, C-3 to C-6 medium, and C-7 to C-9 heavier clubs. Swing weights of D-0 to D-1 are light clubs for most men, D-2 and D-3 medium, and D-4 to D-6 heavy.

Before you buy clubs, take time to talk with one or more golf professionals or trained salespersons. They will give you extensive information. After checking your swing they can make a judgment as to what clubs will

*For detailed information on handicapping and tournaments write the USGA for *Golf Committee Manual* and *USGA Handicap System.*

suit you best. These services are available free-of-charge—you can be an intelligent buyer of clubs that fit you well.

The golf bag you select will depend on the number of clubs you will carry and whether you will carry your clubs and bag on your shoulder or carry them on a cart. Hand carts are popular accessory items. Hand carts and motorized carts can be rented at most courses. Some courses, require players to either rent a motorized cart or hire a caddie. Motorized carts are a boon for those people who could not otherwise play because of walking limitations. Golf purists decry the use of these carts by players who are able to walk the course.

Wearing either a golf glove on the left hand or gloves on both hands will prevent blisters and callouses from forming on the hands, and may also help in holding the club. You will need to wear comfortable, low-heeled oxfords. Golf shoes with spikes are preferred, for these will help you maintain balance in swinging and also will make walking on the course easier. Golf gloves and golf shoes are not absolutely necessary, but they are both recommended. Hats or visors for protection from the sun are also recommended.

Comfortable and appropriate sports clothes should be worn for golf. Complete lines of attractive golf clothes for men and women are sold in many stores, including golf shops at courses.

YOU AND THE GAME OF GOLF

Are You Ready to Attempt Play on the Course?

1. Have you developed some consistency in hitting the ball with the full swing? Do you know the distances you can hit the ball with the various clubs?
2. Have you practiced hitting different distances with the medium and short irons? Have you learned how much to "choke up" on the grip and how much swing to take for given distances?
3. Have you practiced putting so that in most longer putts of 25 feet or more you can hole out in 2 putts? Are you able to sink many putts of 1 to 2 feet in length?
4. Have you carefully studied and learned the safety precautions, etiquette, and the rules? Are you willing to watch the conduct of the experienced golfer and to learn from these observations?

Tips for Your Early Experiences on the Course

1. If available, play a course consisting of short holes. If you play a full-length course, plan to play at a time when the course is not crowded.
2. If possible, have an experienced golfer guide you in correct conduct.
3. You will most likely take more strokes than the experienced golfer. Be willing to make up this time by walking rapidly between shots.
4. Don't be concerned with your scores. Become oriented to the course and follow correct procedure.

5. If you are in a difficult situation, and you may hold up play, consider possible solutions. For instance, finding it impossible to hit from deep rough—pick up your ball, toss it into the fairway and continue play; taking many putts on the green—pick up your ball and discontinue play of this hole.
6. Golf is a complicated game. Be patient. Consider other players. With experience, study, and practice you will soon be playing golf as it should be played.

Golf Conduct

The test of a player is: Does he really play golf? One might think this a ridiculous question. However, golfing authorities are becoming increasingly critical of and concerned about present playing practices. Some people play under the guise: "I play for the fun of it." They do not choose to meet the challenges of the game by playing according to the rules; they have little or no consideration for either their fellow players or the golf course. Although in the minority, their number is great enough to detract from the game and their actions deserve censure. It is hoped that you who have read this book will make some contribution to correcting these poor practices and to preserving the fine traditions of the game.

THE GOLFER'S CODE
Meet the challenges of the game. Play by the rules. The rules are self-enforced.
Be aware of sharing the course with other players. Realize the importance of keeping your place on the course so as not to hold up the play of golfers following.
Follow practices that will help keep the course in the best possible condition. Observe the safety precautions and the etiquette to the finest degree, thereby making play most enjoyable for yourself and for all players.

May your participation in this fine pastime be one of success and pleasure. May your participation and actions show your appreciation of the course and contribute to the recreation and pleasure of all golfers.

glossary
of terms

Ace. A hole in one.

Addressing the ball. Taking the stance and grounding the club, except that in a hazard a player has addressed the ball when he has taken his stance.

All square. A term used in match play to indicate that the match is tied.

Approach shot. A stroke played to the putting green.

Apron. The area surrounding the putting green.

Away. The ball lying farthest from the hole.

Back 9. The last 9 holes of an 18-hole course, also *In 9.*

Backspin. A reverse spin of the ball in the vertical plane.

Banana ball. A slice.

Barranca. A deep ravine. (Spanish)

Bite. The backspin on the ball causing it to stop upon landing on the ground.

Birdie. A score of one under par for a hole.

Bogey. Commonly used to describe a score of one over par for a hole.

Brassie. The 2-wood.

Break of green. The slant or slope of the putting green.

Bunker. Usually a depressed area covered with sand, commonly called a sand trap.

Caddie. A person who carries the clubs and otherwise assists a player as the rules provide.

Casual water. A temporary accumulation of water not recognized as a hazard.

Chip shot. A short, low shot played to the putting green. Also called a run-up shot.

Cup. Term commonly used for the hole on the putting green.

Curtis Cup Matches. International team matches between women amateurs of Great Britain and United States.

Divot. A piece of turf cut or displaced in making a stroke. Should be replaced and pressed down.

Dogleg. A hole in which the fairway curves to the right or left.

Dormie. A term used in match play. A player is dormie when he is as many holes up as there are holes remaining to be played.

Double bogey. A term in common use to describe a score of two over par for a hole.

Double eagle. A score of three under par for a hole.

Draw. A shot that curves slightly in flight from right to left.

Driver. The 1-wood.

Dub. An unskilled golfer; or, to hit a poor shot.

Duffer. A player with poor skill.

Eagle. A score of two under par for a hole.

Explosion shot. A shot played from a sand trap. An attempt is made to swing the club through the sand well back of the ball.

Fade. A shot that curves slightly in flight from left to right.

Fairway. The mowed grassy area between the tee and putting green.

Fat shot. A shot in which the ground is struck before contacting the ball, usually resulting in a poor shot.

Fellow competitor. The person with whom you play in stroke play.

Flagstick. The marker which indicates location of the hole.

Flat swing. A swing in which the club is swung in a low arc. At the top of the backswing the club shaft is lower than the orthodox swing.

Flub. A poorly hit shot; or, to hit a poor shot.

Fore!. A warning cry to anyone who might be endangered by a golf shot.

Foursome. Four players playing together who may or may not be engaged in a match.

Frog hair. The grass surrounding the putting green.

Front 9. The first 9 holes of an 18-hole course, also *Out 9.*

Gross score. The actual total score for a round.

Ground under repair. Staked or lined area on which work is being done. A ball coming to rest in area may be lifted and dropped in accordance with rules.

Grounding the club. Placing the sole of the club on the ground in preparation for making the stroke.

Halved or halving a hole. In match play, to tie a hole.

Handicap. The approximate number of strokes one shoots over par, or the allowance of strokes to equalize players of different ability.

Hazard. By USGA definition, bunkers and water hazards.

High handicapper. A player who shoots many strokes over par, an unskilled player.

Hole. (1) the receptacle on the putting green $4\frac{1}{4}$ inches in diameter and at least 4 inches deep; (2) one unit or division of the course.

Hole high. The ball is in a position as far as the hole but off to either side of it.

Hole out. To complete the play of a hole.

Hook. A ball that curves in flight to the left due to a horizontal, counterclockwise spin on the ball.

Honor. The privilege of hitting first from the tee.

In 9. The second 9 holes of an 18-hole course, also *Back 9.*

L.P.G.A. Ladies Professional Golf Association of America.

Lateral Water Hazard. A water hazard running approximately parallel to the line of play.

Lie. The position of the ball on the ground.

Loft of club. The angle of pitch of the club face.

Loose impediments. Objects such as dead grass and fallen leaves, pebbles, worms, fallen twigs, etc.

Low handicapper. A skilled golfer who shoots near par.

Mashie. The 5-iron.

Match play. Competition based on scores for each hole rather than total score.

Medal play. More commonly called stroke play. Competition by total score.

Medalist. The player with the lowest score for a qualifying round of a match play tournament.

Mid-iron. The 2-iron.

Mixed foursome. A group of four players made up of two women and two men.

Mulligan. An illegal practice of taking a second drive from the first tee without penalty if the first shot is a poor one.

Nassau scoring system. A system of scoring allowing one point to the winner of each 9 holes and one point for the match.

Net score. A score resulting from subtraction of the handicap from the gross score.

Niblick. The 9-iron.

Obstruction. An artificial object on the course which may be movable or fixed.

On the beach. In the sand trap.

Open tournament. A competitive event in which both amateurs and professionals play, such as the United States National Open and the British Open.

Opponent. The player opposing you in a match.

Out 9. The first 9 holes of an 18-hole course, also *Front 9.*

Out of Bounds. Ground on which play is prohibited, usually marked by out of bounds stakes or fences.

P.G.A. Men's Professional Golf Association.

Par. An arbitrary standard of scoring excellence based on the length of a hole allowing two putts on the putting green.

Pin high. Same as hole high.

Pitch shot. A shot that travels in a high trajectory played to the putting green.

Press. Attempting to hit the ball beyond one's normal power.

Pronation. An anatomical term to describe the turning of the hand and forearm inward. Supination is the opposite action in which the hand and forearm are turned out so the palm is facing up.

Provisional ball. A second ball played in case the first ball is or is thought to be lost outside a water hazard or out of bounds.

Pull. A shot that travels to the left of the intended line.

Push. A shot that travels in a straight line, but to the right of the intended target.

Quail high. Low flying shot.

Rainmaker. Shot with a very high trajectory.

Rough. The areas bordering the fairway in which the grass, weeds, etc., are allowed to grow freely.

Royal and Ancient Golf Club of St. Andrews, Scotland. The governing body for golf in Great Britain.

Rub of the green. An unpredictable happening to the ball when the ball in motion or at rest is stopped or deflected by an outside agency.

Ryder Cup Matches. Men's Professional team matches between Great Britain and the United States.

Sand trap. The term commonly applied to a bunker.

Scotch foursome. A foursome of players in which two teams compete. Each team uses only one ball and the players alternate striking the ball.

Scratch player. A player who has a handicap of 0, shooting consistently near par.

Slice. A shot that curves in flight to the right, caused by the ball spinning in a horizontal, clockwise manner.

Spoon. The 3-wood.

Stance. The position of the feet in addressing the ball.

Stroke play. Competition by total strokes.

Stymie. To have another player's golf ball or some object blocking one's line of play—to be stymied. Also an obsolete rule of golf.

Summer rules. The ball must be played as it lies on the fairway, except as otherwise provided by the USGA rules.

Tee. The starting place for a hole; or, the peg on which the ball is placed for driving.

Tee markers. The markers placed on the tee to indicate the forward limits of the teeing area.

Texas wedge. A name applied to the putter when it is used to play any shot from off the putting green.

Through the green. This is the whole of the course, except the teeing ground and putting green of the hole being played and all hazards.

Underclubbing. Using a club that will not give enough distance for the desired shot. For instance, using a 7-iron when a 6-iron or 5-iron should be used —a more common error than overclubbing.

Up and down. Holing out in 2 strokes from off the green.

Upright swing. A swing in which the club is swung high into the air on the backswing and follow-through. The opposite of a flat swing.

USGA. The United States Golf Association—governing body of golf in the U.S.A.

Walker Cup Matches. Matches between men amateurs of Great Britain and the United States.

Whiff. To swing at the ball and miss it completely—to fan.

Winter rules. Special local rules which permit the ball to be moved to a better lie on the fairway; also called "preferred lies."

questions and answers

If you can correctly answer all of the questions in this test, your knowledge of golf is probably above that of the average person playing the game. The questions on rules are arranged so that you can easily check them in the rule book. The rule number is listed and questions relating to that rule follow.

TRUE-FALSE

I. *ETIQUETTE*

1. Your golf course etiquette indicates your consideration for other players on the course.

2. After playing a stroke from a sand trap, a player should smooth out all marks he made in the sand.

3. Players should record their scores on the scorecard before leaving the putting green.

4. No player should play a stroke until the group ahead is out of range.

5. If a group of players fails to keep its place on the course and loses more than one clear hole on the group in front, the slow group should allow the following group to play through.

6. Players while looking for a lost ball have signalled the group following them to pass. Before the second group has passed, however, the ball is found. The first group should hurry and immediately continue play.

7. When attending the flagstick for a fellow competitor, the flagstick should be removed from the hole and held in a position directly back of the cup.

8. All divots should be replaced and pressed firmly in place.

9. Before you tee off from the first tee, be sure to take about six practice swings on the tee in order to warm up properly.

10. Before teeing off from the first tee, members of a foursome should check the names and numbers of the golf balls they intend to use.

11. When playing golf, concentrate on your own game. Do not watch the shots of other players in your group.

12. The approved and best way to identify your ball in play is to pick the ball up from the ground and check the name and number.

13. When your ball is on or near the putting green, place your golf bag on the apron and well off the green preferably on the side of the green nearest the next tee. Do not leave your golf bag at the front of the green.

14. It is good practice and improves your game to take several practice swings before each golf shot you must play.

15. When you hold the flagstick for another player, always stand to the left side of the hole and hold the flagstick and pennant with your right hand.

16. When you play golf, take note of how your foursome is keeping its place on the course. If your group is playing slowly and not keeping its place on the course, you should either urge your group to catch up and maintain its position, or have your group invite the following foursome to play through.

17. Be careful where you stand on the putting green. Do not stand in anyone's line of putt—either in back of the ball or beyond the cup. Also, be certain that your shadow is not cast in the line of play.

18. Chances are that divots dug from the fairway will not grow back, so do not bother to replace them.

19. To hit a good iron shot you must take a divot. So, when you take a practice swing with an iron make sure you take a divot.

20. If you hit your ball into the wrong fairway, you do not have the right-of-way. Before entering that fairway, be certain it is safe to do so, and, be sure you do not bother golfers playing down that fairway.

21. Watch the shot results of the players in your group, so if necessary, you can help in the search for a ball.

22. If a player in your group is having trouble with his game, watch his swing and volunteer some tips to help him improve his strokes.

23. If your ball comes to rest on the wrong putting green, lift the ball from that green. Without penalty, drop the ball off the green within one club length of the nearest point of relief, not nearer the hole.

24. When you enter a sand trap to play a shot, enter at the lowest bank and take the shortest route to the ball.

25. After all players of your foursome hole out, and before you leave the putting green, be certain to check the accuracy of all scores for the hole just played.

26. It is all right to leave your golf bag (or golf bag and cart) at the front of the green, if you hurry to move the golf bag when you have completed play on the green.

27. To speed up play on the course, it is all right to shoot toward the putting green as soon as the players in front have replaced the flagstick in the hole.

28. If you are not putting well, try a few practice putts after your group completes play on each green.

29. When you hold the flagstick for a player, hold both the stick and the banner with the stick remaining in the cup. Stand to one side of the hole and be certain that your shadow is not cast across the player's line of putt.

30. When your group has finished playing a hole, replace the flagstick and leave the green immediately. Do not stand on the green to review play of the hole or to mark your scores on the score card.

31. When your group has been extended the courtesy of playing through another group, you should express your appreciation and proceed with your play without delay.

32. As soon as you hole out your putt, you should remove the ball from the cup.

33. If you hit a ball that is travelling toward someone and may endanger that person, call "FORE!" loudly. At your earliest convenience, express your apology to that person.

34. If players ahead are playing slowly and holding up play, you may prompt them to speed up their play by hitting your shots toward them when you judge they are just moving out of range.

35. Three practices to adopt for care of the putting green are: walk carefully on the green, do not step or stand at the edge of the cup, and repair ball marks on the green.

36. If you tee off first and your drive goes way off line into the wrong fairway or rough, to speed up play, pick up your clubs and hurry to your shot while the other players of your group are teeing off.

37. One player in your foursome is especially deliberate in his preparation for each shot, thus taking a lot of time. There is apparently nothing the other players can do, so you and the other players of the group might as well adopt the same, deliberate style of play.

38. If a player is new to the game and is playing his first rounds of golf, his scores for the early rounds are not so important that his scorekeeping and play should merit holding up the games of other people on the course.

39. It is good practice to mark and lift your ball before each putt you play on the green.

40. When you remove the flagstick from the hole, lay it on the green out of play. Do not drop or throw the flagstick onto the green.

II. RULES

Section 2, Definitions

41. A player has "addressed the ball" when he has taken his stance and grounded the club, except that in a hazard a player has "addressed the ball" when he has taken his stance.

42. "Through the green" includes all of the course except all hazards and the tee and the putting green of the hole being played.

43. If a ball lies so any part of it is touching the green, the ball is deemed to be on the putting green.

44. If out of bounds is fixed by a line on the ground, the line itself is out of bounds. If out of bounds is fixed by stakes, the out of bounds line is determined by the nearest inside points of the stakes at ground level.

45. Sand and loose soil are loose impediments on the putting green only.

Rule 3

46. A player is allowed to carry a maximum of fourteen clubs to play a round.

47. In a friendly game of golf, borrowing a club from another player is common and accepted practice.

48. The rules state specifically that a player may carry not more than fourteen clubs, consisting of one putter, nine irons, and four woods.

Rule 4

49. Golf rules are too complex to master, so in a friendly game where players are out to have fun, the rules may be changed to suit the players.

50. The penalty for waiving a rule is disqualification.

Rule 5

51. Stroke play. A player stamps down the surface of the green in his line of putt. The penalty is two strokes. *(Also Rule 17)*

52. Stroke play. On the fairway. A player pulls out a dandelion growing back of the ball. The penalty is two strokes. *(Also Rule 17)*

53. Stroke play. Before playing his first shot from the teeing area, a player presses down the grass back of the ball. The penalty is two strokes. *(Also Rule 17 and Definition 5)*

54. The general penalty for breach of a rule in stroke play is one stroke.

55. Match play. Before playing a shot from under a tree, a player breaks a small limb from the tree. The penalty is loss of hole. *(Also Rule 17)*

56. Match play. A player grounds his club in a sand trap. The penalty is one stroke. *(Also Rule 33)*

57. The general penalty for breach of a rule in match play is loss of hole.

Rule 6 *(Also Definition 34)*

58. The greatest margin by which a player can win an 18-hole match is 10-8.

59. A player can only win an 18-hole match play round by having a lower total 18-hole score than his opponent.

60. Player A is dormie 2. A loses hole #17, so is now dormie one.

61. A match is tied at the end of 18 holes. To determine the winner, players must continue play until one player wins a hole.

62. Player A is dormie 6. "A" wins the next hole, thus winning the match 7-5.

Rule 7 *(Also Definition 10)*

63. In a stroke play tournament, contestants with whom one plays are called "fellow competitors." In match play competition, the contestant one plays against is called the "opponent."

64. Stroke play. If two or more players are tied for first place at the end of the stipulated rounds, the U.S.G.A. recommends that these players play a round of 18 holes to determine the winner.

Rule 8

65. A practice swing may be taken at any place on the course, provided the player does not violate any rules applying to the area.

66. Match play. During the play of a hole Player A plays a practice shot to the putting green. This player loses the hole immediately.

Rule 9 (Also Definition 2)

67. Match play. Player A asks her opponent, Player B, what club she used for a particular shot. Player B declares that she has won the hole because of the rule violation by A. B is correct.

68. Stroke play. You are allowed to ask your caddie or your fellow competitor for advice.

69. If you are playing a stroke to the putting green and cannot see the flag-stick, you are permitted to ask a member of your foursome to stand in and remain standing in the correct line to the hole, until you play your shot.

70. Stroke play. You ask your fellow competitor's caddie for advice. You are penalized two strokes.

Rule 12 (Also Definition 16)

71. A foursome played from the first tee in this order: A, B, C, and D. The scores for the hole were: A-6, B-4, C-5, and D-4. On the second hole the players should tee off in this order: D, B, C, and A.

72. Stroke play. A player fails to play according to honor. The penalty is two strokes and the ball remains in play.

73. Stroke play. A player fails to play according to honor. There is no penalty and the ball remains in play.

74. Match play. You fail to play according to honor. There is no penalty. Your opponent can either: require you to abandon that shot and play another shot; or, allow you to continue play with the original shot.

75. Match play. You fail to play according to honor. The penalty is loss of hole.

Rule 13 (Also Definition 33)

76. The teeing ground, the starting place for a hole, is a rectangular area extending two club lengths back of the tee markers. The front and sides are defined by the outside limits of the markers.

77. The teeing ground is bounded in front by the tee markers and extends back of the markers one club length.

78. Match play. The penalty for teeing and playing a ball from outside the limits of the teeing area is loss of hole.

79. Match play. There is no penalty for your playing a first stroke from outside the teeing area, but your opponent may require you to replay the shot from within the teeing area.

80. Stroke play. If you play your first stroke from outside the teeing area, the penalty is two strokes. The stroke played from outside the teeing area will not count.

81. Stroke play. Player A plays her first stroke from outside the teeing area. She must count that stroke and then shoot stroke #2 from within the teeing area.

Rule 14 (Also Definition 1 and 5)

82. If in addressing the ball on the tee a player accidentally knocks the ball off the tee, the ball may be re-teed without penalty.

83. If in addressing any golf shot the player accidentally moves the ball, the penalty is one stroke.

Rule 17 (Also Definition 17)

84. If a player's ball comes to rest on sandy soil on the fairway, he is allowed to brush aside the sand back of the ball.

Rule 18 (Also Definition 17)

85. The following are some typical loose impediments: stones (not solidly imbedded); fallen twigs, leaves and branches; worms and insects.

86. Loose impediments may be removed from any place on the course.

87. If you move a loose impediment lying within one club length of your ball on the fairway and the ball moves, the penalty is two strokes and the ball must be played as it lies.

88. Through the green, if you move a loose impediment lying within one club length of your ball and the ball moves before you address it, the penalty is one stroke and you must replace the ball.

89. You may not remove loose impediments from hazards.

Rule 20

90. Player A's ball is on the putting green 60 feet from the hole. Player B's ball is lying off the green 50 feet from the hole. The rules state that Player A should play first because his ball is farther from the hole.

91. Stroke play. A competitor plays his approach shot to the putting green out of turn. The penalty is two strokes.

92. Match play. Your ball is farther from the hole than your opponent's ball, however, your opponent plays before you do. You win the hole.

Rule 21 (Also Definition 5)

93. Stroke play. A player plays a wrong ball from a sand trap and then discovers this mistake. There is no penalty. The player proceeds to play the correct ball and does not count the stroke played with the wrong ball.

94. Match play. Your opponent plays the wrong ball from the fairway. You win the hole.

95. Stroke play. You play the wrong ball from the rough onto the fairway and then discover your mistake. You add two penalty strokes to your score for the hole; you do not count the one stroke played with the wrong ball; then you play the correct ball.

Rule 27

96. If in addressing the ball in play, you accidentally move the ball, the penalty is one stroke and you must play the ball as it lies.

97. Stroke play. Your fellow competitor is helping you search for your ball. He accidentally moves your ball. There is no penalty. You must replace your ball to the spot from which it was moved.

Rule 29 *(Also Definition 6 and 21)*

98. The penalty for hitting a ball out of bounds or for losing a ball outside of a water hazard is two strokes.

99. A player shoots stroke #1 from the tee. He finds the ball in the trunk of a tree and impossible to play. He may go back to the tee and shoot stroke #3; he may drop a ball within two club lengths of the unplayable position, but not nearer the hole and shoot stroke #3; or, he may drop the ball any distance back of the unplayable position (keeping the spot where the ball originally lay between himself and the hole) and shoot stroke #3.

100. A player hits his third shot from the fairway 200 yards from the hole. The ball travels into the rough and after a search, the player declares the ball lost. He may drop a ball on the fairway at the spot where the ball entered the rough and add one penalty stroke to his score for the hole.

101. You hit your drive from the tee. It is obvious that the ball is out of bounds. You must drive again from the tee, and you are shooting stroke #2.

102. You hit your drive from the tee. You are certain it is out of bounds. You must drive again from the tee, and you are shooting stroke #3.

103. The penalty for hitting a ball out of bounds or losing a ball outside a water hazard is one stroke and the player must play his next shot at the spot from which the original ball was played, (stroke and distance penalty).

104. The player is the sole judge as to when his ball is unplayable.

105. A player may stand out of bounds to play a ball that is in bounds.

106. You are allowed 3 minutes to search for a lost ball.

107. You are allowed 5 minutes to search for a lost ball.

Rule 30 *(Also Definition 5)*

108. A provisional ball may be played if a ball may be lost outside a water hazard or may be out of bounds.

109. A provisional ball may be played if a player believes a ball may be lost outside a water hazard, may be out of bounds, or may be unplayable.

110. You hit from the tee and you can see your ball is near the out of bounds fence. You hit a provisional ball from the tee. You find your first ball in bounds, so you continue play with the original ball and pick up the provisional ball. There is no penalty.

Rule 31 *(Also Definition 20)*

111. If out of bounds stakes or out of bounds fences interfere with your play of the ball, you may lift the ball and drop it (according to the rules on dropping a ball). There is no penalty.

(Note: Since the rules regarding dropping the ball may have qualifications, assume in this test that when only the expression "drop the ball" is used that the ball will be dropped according to the rules.)

112. If immovable obstructions such as ball washers, sprinkler heads, benches, protective screens, or paved cart paths, interfere with your stance or the area of your intended swing, you may, without penalty, lift and drop the ball within one club length of the nearest point of relief from the condition, but not nearer the hole.

113. Movable obstructions such as rakes, trash containers, and hoses may always be moved if they interfere with play.

Rule 32 (Also Definition 8 and 13)

114. Through the green (fairway and rough) your ball lies in casual water, or on ground under repair, or in a runway made by a burrowing animal. Without penalty you may lift and drop the ball one club length away, providing relief from the condition, but not nearer the hole.

115. Your ball comes to rest in casual water in a sand trap. The sand trap is completely filled with water so you can only drop the ball outside of the hazard. You must drop the ball in accordance with the rules and add one penalty stroke to your score for the hole.

116. On the putting green casual water is between your ball and the hole. You must either try to putt through the water or putt the ball around the water.

117. If casual water on the putting green intervenes between your ball and the hole, you may lift the ball and *place* it in the nearest position giving you relief but not nearer the hole. There is no penalty.

Rule 33 (Also Definition 14)

118. You hit your tee shot into a water hazard. It is impossible to play the ball. You may play another ball from the tee or you may drop a ball any distance back of the hazard, keeping the spot at which the ball last crossed the margin of the water hazard between yourself and the hole. There is a one stroke penalty.

119. You hit your ball into a lateral water hazard. It is impossible to play the ball. Your only option is to drop the ball within two club lengths of the margin of either side of the hazard, opposite the point where the ball last crossed the hazard. The penalty is one stroke.

120. The penalty for lifting a ball from a water hazard is one stroke. The penalty for losing a ball in a water hazard is two strokes.

121. Stroke play. A player accidentally grounds his club in a sand trap. The penalty is one stroke.

122. Stroke play. A player purposely grounds his club in a sand trap. The penalty is two strokes.

Rule 34 (Also Definition 12)

123. Stroke play. Your ball is three feet off the putting green. You use your putter to stroke the ball and the ball strikes the flagstick. There is no penalty.

124. If you stroke your ball from the putting green and the ball strikes the un-attended flagstick, the penalty is loss of hole in match play and two strokes in stroke play.

125. If you are playing a shot to the putting green and you cannot see the flag-stick, you may have the flagstick held up to indicate the position of the hole.

126. When you are playing a putt from the green you should either request that the flagstick be attended or removed from the cup.

Rule 35 (Also Definition 25)

127. A ball lying on the putting green may be lifted and cleaned without penalty.

128. Any sand, loose soil, or loose impediments may be removed from the putting green. If a player moves the ball in moving such impediments, the ball shall be replaced. There is no penalty.

129. Match play. Both balls on putting green. Player A putts and his ball strikes Player B's ball. Player A loses the hole.

130. Stroke play. Balls on putting green. Your fellow competitor putts and his ball strikes and moves your ball. You must replace your ball to its original position. Your fellow competitor must add two strokes to his score for the hole.

131. You may take any type stance you wish to putt the ball.

132. Match play. Both balls on putting green. Player A putts and his ball strikes and knocks B's ball into the hole. Player A loses the hole.

133. Match play. Par 3 hole. Both players have reached the green in one stroke. Player A putts and his ball strikes and knocks Player B's ball into the hole. Player B scores a one on the hole thereby winning the hole.

134. Stroke play. Par 3 hole. Both players have reached the green in one stroke. Player A putts and his ball strikes and knocks B's ball into the hole. Player B must replace his ball, and Player A is penalized two strokes.

135. Match play. Both balls on putting green. Your opponent's ball strikes your ball and moves it farther from the hole. You may replace your ball. Your opponent is not penalized.

136. Stroke play. Balls on putting green. If your fellow competitor considers that your ball may interfere with her stroke, she may request that you either mark or play your ball at your option.

137. Stroke play. You play your first putt and the ball comes to rest 12 inches from the hole. You may either mark your ball or play it.

138. Stroke play. Putting green. If the ball nearer the hole interferes with play of another ball, the U.S.G.A. recommends that the nearer ball be played rather than lifted, unless subsequent play of a fellow competitor is likely to be affected.

139. Match play. You may concede putts to your opponent.

140. Stroke play. Player A's ball lies 4 inches from the cup. Player B's ball lies 3 feet from the hole. According to the rules Player B may concede the 4-inch putt to Player A.

COMPLETION

141. A score of two under par for a hole is a/an _____ .

142. A score of one over par for a hole is commonly called a/an _____ .

143. A score of one under par for a hole is a/an _____ .

144. A golf shot that curves in flight to the left (for right-handers) is called a/an _____ .

145. The last nine holes of an 18-hole course is called _____ .

146. The first nine holes of an 18-hole course is called _____ .

147. In order for a ball to curve in flight (disregarding any wind factor) the ball must be hit so it spins. In a slice the ball spins _____ .

148. A hole in which the fairway curves to the right or left is called a/an _____ .

149. Par for a hole 375 yards in length is _____ .

150. Par for a hole 200 yards in length is _____ .

151. Par for a hole 525 yards in length is _____ .

152. The general penalty for breach of a rule in stroke play is _____ .

153. The penalty for losing a ball outside of a water hazard is _____ .

154. A player drives his first shot from the tee out of bounds. He tees another ball and drives it out of bounds. He tees a third ball and is shooting stroke number _____ .

155. The total number of clubs a player may carry in a round is _____ .

156. The length of time a player is allowed to search for a ball is _____ .

157. In a correct and effective shot the path of the clubhead through the contact area should be _____ .

158. The most widely used golf grip for all strokes (putting excepted) is the _____ .

159. Your ball is lying in a deep sand trap adjacent to the putting green. There is an overhanging lip on the bunker. Your best choice of club for this shot is _____ .

160. A piece of turf cut or displaced in making a stroke (which should be replaced) is a/an _____ .

161. A stance in which the right foot is placed nearer the intended line of flight than the left foot is called a/an _____ .

162. A stance in which the left foot is placed nearer the intended line of flight than the right foot is called a/an _____ .

163. A second ball played in case the first ball is or is thought to be out of bounds or lost outside a water hazard is a/an _____ .

164. If you can hit a ball 150 yards with a #5-iron, approximately what distance can you expect to hit a ball with a #3-iron? _____ .

165. If you can hit a ball 110 yards with a #7-iron, approximately what distance can you expect to hit a ball with a #5-iron? _____ .

166. Your ball is lying in a sand trap adjacent to the green. The ball is sitting well up on the firm sand, and there is no overhanging turf on the shallow trap. The grass on the apron is cut short. What is your best choice of club for this shot?_____ .

167. Your ball is in a sidehill-uphill lie. You must stand so one foot is higher than the other. Will you play the ball from a spot more opposite the lower foot or higher foot?_____ .

168. In the overlapping, interlocking, or 10-finger grips the V's formed by the thumbs and index fingers should point approximately toward the _____ .

169. The penalty for lifting a ball from a water hazard or losing a ball in a water hazard is _____ .

170. When you finish play of a hole, why should you leave the green immediately and proceed to the next tee?_____ .

171. To hit a straight golf shot to a target, what must the relationship be between the club-face and club path at impact?_____ .

172. You are topping shots with the long irons and fairways woods, but not with the medium irons. What steps would you take to correct the error?

_____ .

173. Joe is playing his first round of golf. His golf ball comes to rest in a deep bunker adjacent to the green. On his fourth attempt to hit the ball from the trap, he hits the ball well past the green into another deep bunker. The foursome following is waiting out on the fairway. What would you do if you were Joe? _____ .

174. You wish to hit a shot so it will curve in flight to the left. By changing your hold on the club you may affect the ball flight. How will you change your hand position for this shot?_____ .

175. You are planning to purchase a minimum set of seven clubs. What is the best selection of clubs you can make for a 7-club set?_____ .

ANSWERS TO EVALUATION QUESTIONS

Page	Answer and Page Reference
3	Tee—area from which first stroke is played for any given hole; fairway—closely mowed grass between tee and putting green; hazards—bunkers (sand traps), creeks and lakes; rough—long thick grass, tree and bush areas; putting green—carpet-like grass surrounding the hole ("Fairway" and "rough" are commonly used terms to distinguish between the closely mowed and long or unmowed parts of that total area defined by the USGA as *through the green*.) (pp. 1-2)
9	Make sure that no one is within striking distance of your club or shot. (pp. 8-9)
13	No, in both cases. (pp. 13, 14)
20	Feet are placed approximately shoulder width apart for long shots; stance is narrower and may be slightly open for short shots. The position of the ball may vary—for long shots play the ball from a point approximately

opposite the inside of the left heel. For short shots play the ball from an area opposite the inside of the left heel extending toward a point opposite the center of the stance. To establish the correct distance from the ball, place clubhead back of the ball with arms easily extended.   (pp. 20-21)

27   The pitch shot is played with a high lofted iron which compresses the ball below center causing backspin. The chip shot, hit with a medium iron, has little or no backspin and a low trajectory. Your skill, condition of the course, contour of the green and cup position, and lie of the ball are factors to consider in deciding which shot to play.   (pp. 27, 32-33)

39   1. Start swing slowly and evenly and accelerate the clubhead gradually.
      2. Key your timing to a medium iron.
      3. Keep same tempo and rhythm for all strokes.
      4. Arms and hands must be attuned to speed at which legs and body can move.
      5. If you have been "rushing" the downswing, the swing may be timed correctly when the downswing "feels" slow.   (pp. 43-45)

46   Answer varies with ability.

51   No answer

54   Reading the green—judging how the ball will roll over the putting surface; hitting the green—reaching the putting green in the par figure alloted; shooting for a birdie—shooting for a score of one under par for a hole; rimming the cup—ball rolls around edge of cup without dropping in.   (pp. 54-55)

55   With skillful putting you can figure that you will take less than 2 putts per hole as allotted by par. You will rarely reach a green in fewer strokes than par allots.   (pp. 54-55)

60   No answer

61   In all three cases most players will aim to the left of the target.

66   No answer

73   Ball will spin counter-clockwise in a horizontal plane and will curve to the left. Hook shot or draw.   (pp. 71-72)

84   Equalization of competition. A handicap is established by playing a given number of rounds and from these scores the handicap chairman of the association or club figures the handicap. A scratch golfer has a handicap of zero.   (pp. 81, 90)

QUESTION ANSWER KEY

True and False

1.	T	29.	T	57.	T	85.	T	113.	T
2.	T	30.	T	58.	T	86.	F	114.	T
3.	F	31.	T	59.	F	87.	F	115.	T
4.	T	32.	T	60.	T	88.	T	116.	F
5.	T	33.	T	61.	T	89.	T	117.	T
6.	F	34.	F	62.	T	90.	T	118.	T
7.	F	35.	T	63.	T	91.	F	119.	F
8.	T	36.	F	64.	T	92.	F	120.	F
9.	F	37.	F	65.	T	93.	T	121.	F
10.	T	38.	T	66.	T	94.	T	122.	T
11.	F	39.	F	67.	T	95.	T	123.	T
12.	F	40.	T	68.	F	96.	T	124.	T
13.	T	41.	T	69.	F	97.	T	125.	T
14.	F	42.	T	70.	T	98.	F	126.	T
15.	F	43.	T	71.	F	99.	T	127.	T
16.	T	44.	T	72.	F	100.	F	128.	T
17.	T	45.	T	73.	T	101.	F	129.	F
18.	F	46.	T	74.	T	102.	T	130.	T
19.	F	47.	F	75.	F	103.	T	131.	F
20.	T	48.	F	76.	T	104.	T	132.	F
21.	T	49.	F	77.	F	105.	T	133.	T
22.	F	50.	T	78.	F	106.	F	134.	T
23.	T	51.	T	79.	T	107.	T	135.	T
24.	T	52.	T	80.	T	108.	T	136.	T
25.	F	53.	F	81.	F	109.	F	137.	T
26.	F	54.	F	82.	T	110.	T	138.	T
27.	F	55.	T	83.	F	111.	F	139.	T
28.	F	56.	F	84.	F	112.	T	140.	F

Completion

141. eagle
142. bogey
143. birdie
144. hook or draw
145. in or back 9
146. out or front 9
147. clockwise
148. dogleg
149. 4
150. 3
151. 5
152. 2 strokes
153. one stroke and distance
154. 5
155. 14
156. 5 minutes
157. from inside the intended line of flight, on the intended line, and inside the
line

158. overlapping grip
159. wedge or high lofted iron
160. divot
161. open stance
162. closed stance
163. provisional ball
164. 170 yards
165. 130 yards
166. putter, or iron to chip the ball from the trap
167. higher foot
168. right shoulder
169. one stroke
170. to avoid delaying play and for your safety
171. clubhead must be travelling on intended line of ball flight with the club-face perpendicular to the line.
172. swing clubhead low to ground, try to hit *low shots*, alternate between hitting shots with the medium irons and longer clubs.
173. pick up the ball and discontinue play of this hole. Resume play at next tee. Better days are coming.
174. right palm facing more skyward, and left palm facing more towards the ground
175. #1 and 3 woods, #3, 5, 7, and 9 irons, and putter

index